TANNENBERG

Perry Pierik

TANNENBERG

*Erich Ludendorff and the
Defense of the Eastern
German Border in 1914*

Aspekt Publishers

TANNENBERG
© 2016 Aspekt Publishers
© 2016 Perry Pierik

Amersfoortsestraat 27, 3769 AD Soesterberg, Nederland
info@uitgeverijaspekt.nl - http://www.uitgeverijaspekt.nl

First print: 2003
Second print: 2016

Cover: Olivier Baron
Interlining: Olivier Baron

ISBN: 9789059111066
NUR: 680

All rights reserved. No part of these pages, either text or image may be used for any purpose other than personal use. Therefore, reproduction, modification, storage in a retrieval system or retransmission, in any form or by any means, electronic, mechanical or otherwise, for reasons other than personal use, is strictly prohibited without prior written permission.

Inhoud

I Introduction **7**

II The downfall of Liege and Ludendorff's appointment in the east **10**

III The battle at Tannenberg **22**

IV Tannenberg, the aftermath **64**

V Epilogue **78**

Situation August 1914.

1.
Introduction

The German commander Erich Ludendorff passed away in Bavaria on the 20th of December 1937. During the last twenty years of his life he had been quite contradictious. Ludendorff had continuously been engaged in a struggle with the world around him since he had married his second wife. Through his own publishing company, which issued a constant flow of books, he did his best to explain the German defeat of 1918. He based his explanation on the *Dolchstosslegende* (stab in the back, literally dagger-stab-legend). The German army hadn't been beaten at the front, but was brought down by destructive forces from within. Ludendorff's criticism was especially directed against Freemasonry, Jesuits and 'international' Jewry. As a result of his radical course Ludendorff alienated from his former colleagues and became more and more isolated. Even Hitler and his rising NSDAP dissociated themselves from Ludendorff, especially because of his anti clerical attitude that could result in losing votes for the nazi's. Despite this bleak end of his life, Erich Ludendorff got a state funeral and condolences were received from all over the world when he died in 1937, shortly before Christmas. This had everything to do with one of his greatest victories, the battle at Tannenberg in 1914.

Tannenberg became the symbol of the successful defence of the German eastern border during 1914 – 1915. Initially it didn't look like it at all that Ludendorff would ever be involved in the defence of the eastern border. The Prussian Ludendorff was regarded a great talent since he was a cadet, but his inflexible character was the reason that he lost his position with the German General Staff in the end. 'Teach this man some discipline' was the order of his superiors when Ludendorff was transferred from headquarters to a position in the field as liaison officer. For years Ludendorff had rightly protested against the changes that, under emperor Wilhelm II, had been made to the 'Schlieffen Plan': it was based on a rapid campaign against France and after it had been defeated it would fully focus on Russia. The German emperor wanted to preserve Alsace-Lorraine from French occupation, which resulted in a German attack with a much weaker right flank.

When the fighting started in August 1914 it was a pure coincidence that Ludendorff was stationed with one of the most important units that had to make the breakthrough on the right flank near Liege. Aware of the iron discipline that would be necessary to defeat France in time, he didn't think twice when the attack near Liege stalled and he personally made sure that this important city and river crossing fell into German hands. This important strategic success was the reason that the - initially critical - army staff rediscovered Ludendorff. And just in time, because in the east the tsarist army had come into action much sooner than expected and threatened to advance to Berlin. Within the concept of the 'Schlieffen Plan' there were no fixed ideas for the battle in the east at this early stage, which meant Ludendorff left for the front carrying a blank cheque. He became the right hand man of Paul von Hindenburg, the silent general who would use his authority to give Ludendorff, his sorcerer's apprentice, all the freedom he needed. This cooperation, during the course of which Ludendorff played first fiddle, became very successful. The first great German success in the east went down into history as the battle at Tannenberg, a name that was chosen by the German command on purpose, because of an earlier historical defeat. Tannenberg became a concept in that period: the defence of the eastern border. The battle at Tannenberg was followed by another series of successes of the German eastern army, such as the battle at the Masurian Lakes, the fights at Lodz and Warsaw, attacks to support the poorly operating Austrian-Hungarian army as well as the winter battle at Masuren in 1915.

In this monograph however we completely focus on the battle at Tannenberg. A battle that has remained a standard in the awareness of the Germans even after the First World War and didn't fade away from their collective memory until the *Wehrmacht*, during its retreat in the Second World War, blew up the monument that commemorated the battle. The interest in the First World War is growing again these days. As a result of the new openness in the east also the battle at Tannenberg is receiving attention again.

II.

The downfall of Liege and Ludendorff's appointment in the east

During the night of the 5th and the 6th of August 1914, around midnight, the men of the 14th infantry brigade from Halberstadt under the command of major general Von Wussow gathered for their march in western direction. While the units assembled, the local commander, general Von Emmich of the 10th army corps, arrived. The general had reasons to be on his way that late. An historical military undertaking was about to start. The 10th army corps had brought five divisions into the field that had marched from their meeting area near Aachen to the fields near Liege. As the forerunner of the larger armies that would follow, it was their task to quickly conquer the strategic city in the valley of the Maas. Von Emmich and Von Wussow were under a lot of pressure as two out of the five armies that had to carry out the 'Schlieffen Plan' would be dependent on the passageway at Liege.

The 'Schlieffen Plan' was the German military answer to the war on two fronts. Assuming that Russia, economically lagging behind, would mobilise slower than Germany, Berlin had decided to use the majority of her forces to crush France first and to take care of the armies of the tsar next. This resulted in tight script of long marches and military objectives that all had to be met. Liege was a dangerous bottleneck.

The Belgian defenders were very well aware of the strategic importance of Liege. By 1914 the city had not only developed into an important centre of industry but was also of major strategic importance because of its location, as an access road and traffic interchange towards the flat north of France. In order to be able to defend the city on the Maas, Brussels had already decided in 1890 to build a number of forts around the city. In the north lay fort Pontisse, east of Wandre fort de Barchon, under Salve fort de Evegnée, just west of Micheroux fort de Fléron and south of the city fort de Chaudfontaine. On the border of the city there was fort La Chatreuse and in the city itself, high upon the hill, the citadel. These magnificent and quite modern forts occupied 6,000 men in times of peace but would be reinforced to 19,000 soldiers during times of war. Floodlights made sure the Belgian defenders would be able to continue fighting even at night and a dozen pieces of artillery in each fort could create major problems for a siege. The commander of Liege was general Léman, who, if time permitted could also place infantry units between the forts, which would create an almost impenetrable line of defence. For this purpose he had been promised 20,000 soldiers. His forces could add up to 30,000 men in total.

Time was the vital element in the 'Schlieffen Plan' and above all played a crucial role in the attack on Liege. With all means Von Emmich had to prevent Léman from bringing in his extra troops. In order to prevent this, his superior, general Von Bülow of the second army of which the tenth army corps was part, had released three cavalry divisions which had to try to cut off the Belgian defenders of Liege from their hinterland, so that reinforcements would be unable to reach the forts and the citadel. Apart from that, the five brigades that assembled during the night of the 5th and the 6th would have to sneak in between the forts to take the city and citadel by surprise. In total Von Emmich had 25,000 infantry and 8,000 cavalrymen available to him, as well as 124 pieces of artillery although these would be of little value during a nightly assault.

The 14th brigade of Von Wussow looked somewhat disoriented when it assembled near Micheroux. The soldiers were 27 kilometres away from the safe town of Aachen and it seemed they still had to get used to the idea of war. The troops of Von Wussow were very vulnerable at that time. While they assembled, the German officers kept looking towards the west, at fort de Fléron from where they could open fire any moment. The swiftly increasing German troops were an easy prey now. But by a miracle nothing happened and at 1,00 am Von Wussow gave the orders to advance. The air was filled with tension when they passed the fort, but nothing happened and it would not be the only miracle that happened near Liege. The 10th army corps advanced quickly now towards Rentinne. The brigade was now located exactly in the middle of the German attack. The 27th and 34th brigade operated in the north and from the south Liege was approached by the 11th, 38th and 43rd.

Somewhere at the back of the column of Von Wussow's men was the command post of Von Emmich. Erich Ludendorff, who had been appointed liaison officer between the 10th army corps and the 2nd army of Von Bülow, was in his company. This made Ludendorff a *Schlachtenbummler* as he called it, an officer without any troops under his command, a commuter between two headquarters. But he found himself in the centre of the 'Schlieffen Plan' and he was fully aware of that. Between Rentinne and La Chartreuse, in the hills in front of the city, the German advance got into trouble. The column couldn't move forward anymore and Von Emmich got stuck in the convoy. Ludendorff immediately offered to have a look to see what was going on, something that Von Bülow was also eager to know and he left Von Emmich to move forward. It turned out the soldiers had lost contact with the troops up front and had stopped near Rentinne without any valid reason. Ludendorff immediately understood the danger and took the initiative although he wasn't a commanding officer. It was pitch-dark when the soldiers entered Rentinne. But when they arrived in town the troops got disoriented. Ludendorff and his men left the town using a different way than planned and walked straight into a rain of bullets. 'Never will I forget the sound of bullets hitting bodies' Ludendorff wrote in his memoirs. Ludendorff had to take his units back into Rentinne, something which was against his honour as a soldier - 'they probably thought I was a coward' – but something else was far more important. When Ludendorff finally found the correct road, he met the adjutant of Von Wussow there, with the horse of the commander. Ludendorff had to accept another setback. The young man told him that Von Wussow had been killed.

This turned out to be true. With the few soldiers he had with him, Ludendorff now took the right road in the direction of Queue du Bois and ran into the lifeless bodies of his comrades. At that moment the Belgian artillery opened fire. Ludendorff escaped from being killed. Ludendorff had not only found the right way but also went ahead in battle. This battle became more and more chaotic. Units of the 4th and 27th brigade were running all over the place. It was very important now to regain initiative. Through the gardens of the town some officers managed to creep up on the Belgian artillery and to eliminate them. At dawn Ludendorff shot, with the help of supplied artillery, the last remains of Belgian resistance into flames. Shortly afterwards the German troops stood on the hills of Chartreuse with Liege lying beneath them, a large grey town and its citadel.

Ludendorff was very worried. The soldiers were tired, field kitchens had been left behind and morale wasn't very good after the chaotic fights during the night. Ludendorff organised food from civilian homes and tried to encourage his soldiers. He also gave Liege a foretaste by shooting a grenade into the city once in a while, to make the Belgians ready for negotiations. It was bluff poker, even more than Ludendorff realised. He only had a few troops that were very tired, some artillery and little ammunition at his disposal but what was even worse was the fact that the other brigades had not yet been able to reach the fields near Liege. Not everybody had been so lucky with a silent fort such as de Fléron.

The liaison officer Ludendorff hesitated between action and consolidation. The 'Schlieffen Plan' was clear: tempo, if need be driving the enemy away with bayonets. But that was easier said than done. An additional problem was the number of Belgian prisoners of war that now reached one thousand. Suddenly the white flag was hoisted over the citadel of Liege. Ludendorff consulted with Von Emmich. 'Wait until they send a negotiator' was Ludendorff's advice, but Von Emmich decided to send *Hauptmann* Von Harbou over for negotiations. A lot of time had been lost when it became clear that the flag had been hoisted without the permission of the Belgian commander. 'A heavy night lay ahead of us', Ludendorff wrote after the war.

In the meantime Ludendorff had sent some scouts to the back to get some clarity on his position. This was bad news. Nobody came back and no new orders came through. It looked like his little unit stood in front and alone at the banks of the Maas. If Léman would attack, the Belgian troops would simply crush the small forces of Ludendorff. Ludendorff 'parked' his Belgian prisoners of war in fort La Chartreuse, which wasn't occupied by the Belgians. He had the relative large Belgian group guarded by only one company, whose commander looked at him as if Ludendorff had lost his mind. But these were emergency situations and Ludendorff had to take risks. That same evening he ordered *Hauptmann* Ott to conquer the bridge over the Maas so that the assault on Liege could start the next morning.

The campaign of August 1914 was all about time, but didn't develop like the 'Blitzkrieg' of 1940. Even after this performance that was far from fortunate, Ott managed to establish a bridgehead on the west bank of the Maas. Belgian troops surrendered on the way. The next morning Ludendorff followed with the majority of his men. *Oberst* Von Oven had been given the order to conquer the citadel. This was the last crucial bulwark in the city. A fierce defence could lead to a collapse of the already shaky operation of Von Emmich and would have enormous consequences for the German script. It is remarkable that something went wrong again. Von Oven's troops did not attack the citadel but turned, for reasons still unknown, into the direction of fort Loncin. When Ludendorff arrived by car in Liege later on and heard no more shooting at the citadel, he thought Von Oven had already conquered it. He drove to the gate and was surprised there was nowhere a German in sight. That didn't keep him from banging on the door with his staff after which an astonished Belgian defender opened the door. Ludendorff wasn't embarrassed at all, went inside and demanded, with a loud voice, their capitulation. By then units of the brigade were approaching the citadel and the Belgian defenders lost their courage. The incredible happened, the citadel surrendered and hundreds of Belgian soldiers were taken prisoner. Ludendorff, a liaison officer without any soldiers became the hero of Liege.

It turned out that hundreds of German soldiers were locked up in the citadel, taken prisoner during the attempts of other German brigades. The different units these soldiers belonged to had convinced Léman that a large number of German forces was waiting at the gates of the city, after which a considerable part of the defenders of Liege had moved back to the west in order to prevent destruction. Léman had hoped for a tough defence by the ones that had stayed behind, but they thought differently. According to a Belgian historian these troops mainly consisted of reserves and they were badly organised. The severe looks of Ludendorff were sufficient to break down moral. Immediately after this, the German units took over the citadel and equipped it for defensive purposes. The Maas had been crossed successfully and the passageway through Liege had been secured. The other forts around Liege were now blown to pieces by the artillery that had been able to advance. These were sometimes heavy fights, but no longer in the eye of the storm. That lay in removing this huge danger to the 'Schliefen Plan'. '*Der weitere Weg war frei*', Ludendorff wrote after the war and he was right.

Ludendorff and Von Emmich were awarded the *Pour le Mérite*, the *Blaue Max*, a desired military decoration. But what was far more important, was the fact that military history had been made during the night of the 5th and 6th of August. A military success had been achieved that wouldn't be repeated until Eben Emael in May 1940 and a career had been born against all odds, the career of Erich Ludendorff. The officer had started his long journey that would take him from the battlefields of World War One to the *Feldhernnhalle* in Munich where he associated his name and fame with a politician who was to become one of the most powerful and feared men of the century: Adolf Hitler. Ludendorff and his superiors started to believe in his mission, one he had, long and lonely, worked and fought for. The fact this mission originated from a mixture of chaos, luck and blunders, as happened so often in (military) history, was quickly forgotten. What if the Belgians had blown up the bridge across the Maas, what if Léman had gathered his men and had made them go back to Rentinne? What if only one Belgian soldier had fired his weapon after Ludendorff had knocked on the door. The Belgian historian Sophie de Schaepdrijver pointed out recently that also a pro-German treason has been of major importance in this case. A Belgian who worked for the Germans had given the order to evacuate a number of forts around Liege, precisely in the sector where Ludendorff operated. The spy was caught and shot later on, but damage had already been done. This anecdote probably belongs to the secret history of World War One, as it is neither mentioned in Ludendorff's war memories nor in the majority of its literature.

'Liege was a special favour of destiny', Erich Ludendorff thought, looking back at his adventurous and fortunate start of World War One. As a result of Ludendorff's firm actions the citadel had fallen into German hands without many problems. The right wing of Von Schlieffen and Von Moltke could start with the 'revolving door'. While units marched ahead, the heavy artillery that Von Schlieffen had dictated after the siege of Tours was rolled forward. These were very heavy mortars, partly borrowed from the Austrian-Hungarian army and partly manufactured by their own Krupp factories, which had to eliminate the strong fortifications around Liege. Ludendorff witnessed the bombardment of fort de Pontiffe and fort Loncin, in which the Belgian commander Léman had been entrenched. Already earlier fort Bachon had been taken and fort Chaudfontaine had partly exploded. The enormous grenades went so slowly that you were able to follow them with your eyes. The effect was just as spectacular as it was horrible. The third grenade that was fired at fort Loncin hit the ammunition depot. The concrete fortress literally exploded. The Belgian soldiers were completely blackened when they crawled from the remains and cried 'don't kill us', which surprised Ludendorff: 'But we aren't barbarians'. Soon the fortifications were no longer an obstacle. 'My heart felt a lot lighter'

Ludendorff wrote in his *Kriegserinnerungen*.

The German press reported proudly about the accomplished results. They even talked about the 'Secret of Luttich', so easily had the heavy fortifications been brought down. 'Hurrah in Liege' Von Emmich had telegraphed home and emperor Wilhelm II had kissed Von Moltke on both cheeks. Hurrah-patriotism broke loose intensely. It was proudly reported that even a zeppelin had been brought into action during the attack on Liege. This sounded much more exciting than it actually was, the first bomb that was thrown out of a zeppelin (*Luftkreuzer nr. 6*) on enemy target (Liege) had been a dud. The next ones did explode, but you could hardly call it a bombardment with precision. In total around 4500 Belgian soldiers were taken prisoner. Among them was the 64 years old commander of Liege, the proud general Léman, with his impressive long moustache. He was found, almost choked to death, under the remains of fort Loncin that had been destroyed by a 42 cm mortar and was taken prisoner. The German generals met with the poor general, gave him something to drink and praised his brave defence. General Von Emmich even handed him back his sabre, like gentlemen amongst each other and as a token of 'German chivalrousness'. Léman had not expected this and was visibly moved. After a medical examination Léman was taken to Magdeburg where he went into captivity. From there he wrote an emotional letter to the Belgian king in which he explained that he had fought to the bitter end and only had been taken prisoner, instead of fallen in battle, because he had lost consciousness. He asked the king forgiveness.

The German losses were limited, although among the

persons killed were *Prins* Friedrich Wilhelm zu Lippe, a descendant from the ruling house zu Lippe and *Generalmajor* Karl von Bülow, the youngest brother of the chancellor. The French reports in the press about German losses of 20,000 men were exaggerated. Von Stein, Von Moltke's right hand man, was eulogistic about the accomplished results. 'Every expert can understand the magnificence of this achievement', he said. In the meantime, Liege had been put under German military rule. The commander of the city *Generalmajor* Bayer tried, in cooperation with mayor Kleyer, to start up normal life again.

There was little time for Ludendorff to enjoy this first spectacular success. Marching was required! The iron script of military logic had begun. On the 21st of August Ludendorff was standing on the banks of the Sambre and saw men of the 2nd Guard division cross the river at Namur. The following day he was on his way to Germany again. He had been summoned. There was a new assignment waiting for him…in the east! He said goodbye to general Von Emmich and his chief of staff *Graf* von Lambsdorff, who he had learned to appreciate during the short time they had worked together. Via hotel Union in Aachen on his way to Coblenz, to the headquarters of the General Staff of the army ('Oberste Heeresleitung = OHL'). On his way back he saw houses burning in the night. The modern war already showed its first element of its frightfulness.

Meanwhile Von Emmich had been nominated for the high decoration *Pour le Mérite*. A few days later it was Ludendorff's turn. For Ludendorff it was obvious that Von Emmich, being the highest in command, received the decoration first, but the fact that he didn't receive his decoration until he was in Coblenz, from emperor Wilhelm II himself, made it clear to him he still had enemies at headquarters. In his war memories Ludendorff bravely remarked that the success at Liege had not been the work of only one person, but that more men had to share the fame. But all of that did not alter the fact that Ludendorff, being kicked upstairs, had placed himself in the centre of attention again by conquering the citadel of Liege at a decisive moment in the 'Schlieffen Plan'. In Coblenz they were now also convinced that the nuisance Ludendorff could also mean 'trouble' for the enemy, and because of that, be an asset to the country that was unexpectedly being threatened. In spite of the positive reports from Liege, there were serious problems in the east.

III.

The battle at Tannenberg

The tsarist troops in the east had come into action much sooner than expected and now threatened large parts of Prussia. There was even panic. The 'Schlieffen Plan' and the 'Moltke II Plan' were not expecting such a quick reaction from the Russians. Ludendorff had received a cry for help from headquarters in Coblenz: 'We have no other person we can trust, maybe you can still save the situation in the east', it said hardly hopeful. The letter signed by Von Moltke's right hand man Von Stein, also said that they realised that by taking Ludendorff away from the western front, they removed him from the decisive phase and location of the 'Schlieffen Plan'. 'You have to bring this sacrifice for the fatherland', Von Stern said, who hoped that Ludendorff 'would not be angry about this'. 'It is a difficult task, but you will succeed', Von Stein concluded encouragingly. This letter, which was confirmed by *Oberstleutnant* A.D. Theobald von Schaefer, historian of the *Reichsarchiv*, in 1927, is authentic and a genuflection of the OHL for Ludendorff, the man who 'had to be taught some discipline'.

Ludendorff arrived at the OHL in Coblenz at 06,00 pm.

From one of his subordinates, captain Von Rockow, Ludendorff had learned that he had to take over the command in the east, reporting to Von Hindenburg, where the German 8th army had run into problems at Gumbinnen against the Russian Njemen army under the command of Von Rennenkampf. Although Ludendorff regretted that he could no longer be part of the decisive days in the west, his thoughts were now fully in the east: Thorn, Kulm, Graudenz and Posen. His footsteps lay everywhere, it was his native soil. He was proud of the words of recognition in Von Stein's letter. He was deeply moved when the emperor pinned on the *Pour le Mérite* and complimented him; 'These are my proudest and most emotional memories of the war'.

Immediately after this duty called again. A special train with Ludendorff on board left for the east at 9,00 pm. Coblenz, the city where Rhine and Mosel meet, was left behind to start a new adventure. For Ludendorff the survival of *Deutschtum* was at stake. At 4,00 am in the morning of the 23rd of August he met *General der Infantrie* Paul von Beneckendorff and Von Hindenburg on the platform of the railway station of Hannover. Von Hindenburg was an impressive appearance, although – sent straight to the front from retirement – he looked rather peculiar in his peace uniform that didn't fit him that well anymore as a result of all those kilos of bacon. But Von Hindenburg, born in West Prussia in 1847, was a happy man. As a former serviceman he was ashamed of having to sit at home during wartime and he had eagerly accepted his appointment. Von Hindenburg had a lot of experience. He had even experienced the battle at Koniggratz in 1866 in the capacity of adjutant. He retired in 1911 but now started, at the age of 66, with his second career. He had insisted on it. After his years in the service, he and his wife had retreated to Hannover, dreaming of a future quiet autumn of their life on an estate in Neudeck. But Von Hindenburg revived every time his son Oskar came home with his buddies from the army. Oskar Von Hindenburg served with the 3rd Infantry Guard Regiment, a unit in which Von Hindenburg had also served. He enjoyed their stories, as well those of his son-in-law who served with the dragoons. When the war broke out he wrote the General Staff: 'If you need somebody, don't forget me. I am mentally and physically fit'. When the OHL sounded him out in the end, Von Hindenburg's answer had been concise: '*Bin bereit!*' (I'm ready).

It was the first time they met. According to Von Hindenburg's biographer Wolf. J. Buetow both men liked each other from the beginning. They spoke the same military language, both were infantrymen and from Prussian descent. Their difference in age, Ludendorff was seventeen years younger, was no issue. After a short meeting, which lasted thirty minutes, Von Hindenburg proposed to get some sleep. Ludendorff agreed, but with his restless mind, which was hiding behind his formal austere appearance, sleep will not have come easily whereas Von Hindenburg gladly placed any earthly concerns into God's hands. It was this, at all times calm, figure in the background who would assist the sensitive Ludendorff in achieving his fame as a soldier, but ultimately wouldn't be able to prevent his failure as a result of this same characteristic.

The German army in the east was initially under the command of *Generaloberst* von Prittwitz und Gaffron and his chief of staff Von Waldersee. The 66 years old Von Prittwitz, nicknamed *Der Dicke*, was notorious for his vanity and thanked his career, according to historian Barbara W. Tuchman, more to his flair and the way he presented himself to the emperor than to his military capacities. Von Moltke had his doubts about 'his man' in the east from the start. To keep an eye on everything, Von Moltke had sent his confidant Von Waldersee over to join Von Prittwitz's staff. But Von Walsersee had recently been operated and wasn't fit. Within the staff Von Moltke had to fall back onto 1st staff officer colonel Max Hoffmann.

In defence of Prussia Von Prittwitz had the 8th army at his disposal; it consisted of the 1st army corps (Von Francois), the 17th army corps (Von Mackensen), the 20th army corps (Von Scholz), the 1st reserve corps (Von Below) and a number of other units, such as the 3rd reserve division (Von Morgen), three brigades of the *Landwehr* and the garrisons of the *Weichselfestungen* Thorn and Graudenz as well as the *Ostseefestung* Königsberg (today Kaliningrad) and some other small fortified towns. They defended an area that was split into two parts by the Masurian Lakes. Von Schlieffen had already pointed out the strategic possibilities of this geographical fact. During an attack the Russian army would be split in two. This was reinforced by the fact that fortress Lötzen was located in between these lakes, like a golf breaker that sticks far out into the sea. Air reconnaissance units and Jewish-Polish spies tried to supply the German army with information.

Shortly after the break out of the war Von Prittwitz had gotten into trouble. In spite of all the legitimate criticism on Von Prittwitz, an incorrect light has often been shed on his first actions in East Prussia. In various publications it is often suggested that Von Prittwitz attacked the Russians in a harebrained way directly after Von Rennenkampf had lined up his army in East Prussia. That is not correct. Von Prittwitz, who moved his headquarters to Bartenstein on the 16th of August, was actually getting ready for the 'border battle' and consequently wanted to install his troops behind the river Angerapp, but he overlooked the wilfulness of Von Francois of the 1st army corps. Von Francois originated from a military family in Normandy. His grandfather had been an Schill-warrior and his father Bruno Francois was killed on the 6th of August 1870 during the French-Prussian war. This very competent officer didn't at all consider the idea of waiting for the Russians all the way behind the Angerapp and advanced already to the east on the 16th, past Gumbinnen in the direction of the Russian border. That same day Von Prittwitz ordered him to immediately stop his isolated advance without any cover on the flank, but the 58 years old hothead, whose ancestors had been Huguenots, reported he wanted to stop the Russians as close as possible near the border in order not to give up any territory. It was a painful surprise to Von Prittwitz that Von Francois was serious about that. On the 17th his corps had reached Stallupönen, close to the Russian border. That same day Von Rennenkampf's army came into action, two days after Japan joined the allies, thus safeguarding the Russian border in the east. An enormous army approached Von Francois over the full length of the front. But for the time being luck was on his side. In his sector, where the Russian 3rd corps was located, consisting of the 25th and 27th infantry division under the command of general Jepantschin, the Russians had lined up a little bit too early because of coordination errors. Von Francois was confronted with a limited force and took his chance. From the church tower of Stallupönen he immediately led his troops, the 1st infantry division (Von Conta), the 2nd infantry brigade (Paschen), and the 2nd infantry division (Von Falk), into battle. Especially the 27th Russian infantry division was caught by surprise by the attack just east of Stallupönen. The Russians were thrown back and Von Francois proudly reported that 3,000 Russians had been taken prisoner.

So the battle of East Prussia had started with a tactical victory of the 1st corps of Von Francois, right at the border. But Von Francois was in great danger, because the troops of Von Rennenkampf had started to move along the entire front now. Von Prittwitz informed Von Francois by telephone that he had to retreat immediately in the direction of Gumbinnen. Von Francois had the following reply sent back: 'Inform general Von Prittwitz that general Von Francois will retreat after he has beaten the Russians.' Von Prittwitz directed his staff officer Grünert forward to see whether Von Francois would follow his orders. Although Von Francois withdrew his troops in the direction of Gumbinnen in the end, the situation had now drastically changed. The Germans had smelled blood and now also Von Prittwitz thought about an earlier counter attack. Considering the whole situation, Max Hoffmann takes the view that the actions of Von Francois were understandable but wrong. His self-willed actions indeed led to German overconfidence. The Russian advance of the 19th and 20th of August was hesitantly, partly because of problems with their transport troops and also because Von Rennenkampf, noticing that Samsonov who was operating south of the lakes fell into line slowly, wanted to keep pace. The most decisive argument of Von Prittwitz, which tempted him to a counterattack at an earlier stage, was the fact that as a result of Von Francois actions there wasn't a closed front at the Angerapp anymore, which meant he couldn't carry out his original plan. A dangerous and for Von Prittwitz fatal scenario unrolled now.

Von Prittwitz decided to give it a chance. At first the operation seemed to go well. On the 20th of August good news was received in Coblenz: the 8th army at Gumbinnen had launched its attack. There was also good news from the front in the west, the German troops in Alsace-Lorraine made good progress and the right wing of the German army was entering Brussels. But in the evening of the 20th Von Prittwitz had to revoke the positive news. It seemed that Russian reinforcements had arrived from Warsaw and he withdrew his troops in western direction. The attack at Gumbinnen had among others been carried out by the troops of August Von Mackensen. Von Mackensen was a passionate soldier who was very keen to protect Prussia from a Russian invasion. But he also realised the limitations of the German army that was relatively weak in the east. 'I foresee a long war' he wrote to his wife, 'it is all or nothing'. The attack developed far from positive. The Russian artillery, feared for years, welcomed the, with a lot of bravado, attacking German troops, which suffered heavy losses. Another reason for the problems of Von Mackensen was, according to Max Hoffmann, the fact that the German troops went too quickly into battle after they had chased away the Russian reconnaissance patrols. Without a solid preparation of the artillery Von Mackensen had come across positions that were well prepared. The exact losses are unknown, but fluctuate between 8,000 and 9,000 men, around 7,000 with Von Mackensen and 2,000 with Von Francois. Von Mackensen was quite relieved when he received the orders of the commander of the 8th army, Von Prittwitz, to withdraw. But the retreat almost immediately turned into a flight. Soldiers of the 35th division of Von Mackensen had fled and even thrown away their weapons. The situation became a lot more dramatic than the one at Stallupönen. This time the Russian achieved a tactical victory. 'Those who have fallen are a true example of the courage of the German soldier', Von Mackensen wrote in his diary. While the situation at Gumbinnen deteriorated, pressure also increased on the 20th corps south of the Masurian Lakes. Von Prittwitz informed the OHL in Coblenz that a normal retreat wouldn't be sufficient and that he wanted to withdraw behind the river Weichsel.

On the 21st of August there was contact between the OHL and Prittwitz and in the evening Moltke succeeded in talking with Von Prittwitz directly, using primitive communication lines. It became clear that Von Prittwitz didn't believe in a fight east of the Weichsel anymore. Even worse, Von Prittwitz told Moltke that he doubted whether they would be able to keep the line of defence at the Weichsel with these weak units.

It was now clear to the OHL that Von Prittwitz was mentally broken by this setback. Max Hoffmann rightly makes the remark in his memoirs *Der Krieg der versäumten Gelegenheiten* (The War of the Missed Opportunities) that the opportunity of the defenders of Prussia to withdraw behind the Weichsel was a serious psychological danger for the 'weaker personalities', by which he obviously meant Von Prittwitz. It was Von Prittwitz first experience at the front, while both his Russian counterparts were veterans from the Russo-Japanese war. Independent leaders who perceived the current problems in the east as an assignment for the fatherland were required. Von Moltke pushed Von Hindenburg forward and also Ludendorff could count again on the close attention of the General Staff. They had to win as much time as possible in the east so that the 'revolving door' in the west could continue its work. But were there still possibilities east of the Weichsel? Max Hoffmann thought there were. In fact in his memoirs, which were published in 1923, he isn't that negative about Gumbinnen. Gumbinnen had mainly been a setback for Von Mackensen, the other units weren't in such a bad shape at that time. Victory was near, according to Hoffmann, until the message was received, through the general of the artillery Von Scholz, that Samsonov had become active south of the lakes. At that moment Max Hoffmann and Grünert both were at the headquarters in Ortelsburg. 'I fear that the nerves of the Commander in Chief will not stand up against this news', Hoffmann told Grünert. 'I would rather not pass on the message, we could then finish the battle (successfully) tomorrow and focus ourselves on the Warsaw army (Samsonov)'. Grünert pointed out to Hoffmann that it would be impossible to withhold this important information from Von Prittwitz and Hoffmann realised that. The revenge on the temporary setback at Gumbinnen escaped the Germans as a result of this, according to Hoffmann, but claimed at the same moment that the re-alignment of Von Prittwitz troops, which followed after this report, already formed the prelude to Tannenberg's victory. To the left or to the right, Hoffmann was sure about victory from the beginning, but that was in 1923 when he published his memoirs and it's always easy from hindsight. Besides, he wouldn't have liked to go down in history as a loser who served under Von Prittwitz and he saw himself under both commanders as the spiritual father of Tannenberg. The changing of the guards went quite rude. The staff officers knew earlier about the replacement of Von Prittwitz than he did. He suppressed his disappointment and said good-bye with dignity.

On the 24 of August Ludendorff and Von Hindenburg arrived in Rastenburg – where Hitler was to have his *Wolfsschanze* headquarters later on – for a meeting with the officers of the 20th army corps that was located south of the Masurian Lakes. According to Hoffmann Von Hindenburg would become a 'demigod' later on, but at that moment he was a relatively unknown officer. Hoffmann met him for the first time. Ludendorff on the other hand had been the talk of the town since Liege. His efforts to get the army in good shape before the war were also widely known. Ludendorff and Hoffmann had also lived in the same building in Berlin for four years and had been stationed in Posen together. Therefore it was Hoffmann who informed the newly arrived officers about the situation at the front. Von Scholz was nervous and hesitated whether his troop would be able stand firm when Samsonov would deploy all his troops. It was clear that also Von Scholz, like Von Prittwitz, felt for moving to the west. Ludendorff ended this discussion immediately. Stand firm until the last man, was his assignment to the 20th army corps. He pointed out that the 1st army corps of Von Francois, after an emergency transport by train from the northern sector via Königsberg – Marienburg, would join the 20th army corps in the south and that the lines of Von Below would be strengthened with troops from the *Weichselfestungen* (Vistula fortresses).

Ludendorff understood the situation well. Aware of the weak plight of the right wing in the west, he realised that the vision of Von Prittwitz, to stand firm on the Weichsel until assistance arrived from the west, was possibly too optimistic. The eastern front had to do it on its own for the time being and maintain operational space. Ludendorff decided for a renewed attempt east of the Weichsel. Already from Coblenz, 1,000 kilometres from the front, he ordered the units north of the lakes to stop their hastily retreats towards the Weichsel. At first he let them hold the line for a while after which he made them turn south. This made clear what Ludendorff was up to. He made the decision to take care of the 2nd Russian army of Samsonov south of the Masurian Lakes first, taking full advantage of the geographical conditions of the area. Samsonov was known as one of the most talented Russian officers. He was new on the western front but had gained war experience as commander of a cavalry division during the war of 1904-1905 against Japan. On his 43rd Samsonov was made general. In 1909 he had been governor of Turkestan until he was asked to report to Warsaw during the mobilisation where he got the command over the 2nd army. Ludendorff opted for the *Entscheidungsschlacht* (decisive battle), a victory that would give the Germans in the east room to breath for a longer period of time in order to cope with possible setbacks on the western front. This was a very ambitious plan.

The *Entscheidungsschlacht* didn't start offensively, but

with defensive battles and complex regroupings. Ludendorff's long experience in calculating stages came in very handy now. The southern flank, the 1st and 20th corps, had to stop the advance of Samsonov, while the most important units of the plagued northern front, Von Mackensen and Von Below, had to move south using forced marches and Von Francois was moved by train. Ludendorff, supported by his superior Von Hindenburg who approved all his plans, took an enormous risk in doing this. Not only were the garrisons of the *Weichselfestungen* already 'used up', but also the flank north of the Masurian Lakes became dangerously uncovered. Ludendorff tried to camouflage this by using the 1st cavalry division, which tried to give the troops of Von Rennenkampf the impression there was still a closed German front facing them.

The balance of power along the entire front was strongly in favour of the Russian northwest front, which also consisted of the troops under the command of Von Rennenkampf and Samsonov. This front was under the command of Shilinski, general of the cavalry, assisted by his chief of staff, Dranovski. In total the Russians had 540,000 men and 1600 pieces of artillery at their disposal; in units: 21 infantry divisions and 10 cavalry divisions that is 354 battalions and 331 squadrons. The German army was able to face them with 180,000 men and 600 pieces of artillery. These numbers didn't make the German chances look very positive. Ludendorff's measures nevertheless turned out to have a positive effect on the soldiers. The soldiers in the east, most of them were of Prussian descent, were very keen not to give up the homeland to the Russian invaders. This had also impelled them to launch the passionate assault at Gumbinnen. But their morale had been affected by losing this battle. The retreat towards the west that followed had just made it worse. But Ludendorff had barely arrived or a new order was received at the staff of the 20th corps: 'stop the retreat towards the west, march to the south!' Major Von Schwerin of the staff of the 20th corps brought the message straight to Von Mackensen. A feeling of relief took possession of the troops, apparently there was still a chance, Gumbinnen might only have been a setback. 'I remember the cheerful atmosphere that suddenly developed', Von Schwerin remembered. '*Die Neue Parole: heran an den feind!*' ('The new slogan: forward on the enemy'), major Von Winning of the 36th infantry division wrote in his memoirs.

The regrouping of the German forces on the northern wing started under cover of the 1st cavalry division. The 1st reserve corps reached the area around Seeburg on the 25th of August, after a march of 35 kilometres in the heat and over roads filled with refugees. The troops of Von Mackensen, having lost more than 200 officers at Gumbinnen, had to cover an even longer stage but succeeded in marching 50 kilometres in southern direction. Everything seemed to be well on the northern front after all.

The real problems occurred with Von Scholz. While Von Rennenkampf was also gasping for breath after Gumbinnen, Samsonov's troops were moving in western direction, quite fresh. Ludendorff had to bring this advance to a halt if he wanted to corner Samsonov's forces south of the Masurian Lakes, between the approaching units of Von Below and Mackensen on one side and those of Von Francois and Scholz on the other. 'Hang on, hang on!' was therefore the motto, while every man, every cannon was brought to the point of departure of the *Entscheidungsschlacht*. Even the *Landwehr*-brigade that was stationed at the lonely fortress of Lötzen was added to the northern forces.

Meanwhile the 20th army corps had to do its utmost. Between the 23rd and 24th of August the fighting intensified in the area between Frankenau, Lahna and Orlau, near the river Alle. The 37th infantry division under the command of *Generalleutnant* von Staabs, which got stuck between the 70th *Landwehr*-brigade and the 3rd reserve division of *Generalleutnant* von Morgen came under the highest pressure. Apart from these the forces of Von Scholz that had to slow down Samsonov consisted of the 41st infantry division (*Generalmajor* Sontag) and the Unger division under the command of *Generalmajor* Fritz Unger, consisting of various garrisons that had been scraped together. The 37th division found itself in the thick of the fight. This division had to defend an area with a frontline that was 12 kilometres long, which was really too much for only one division. In Frankenau it came to heavy fights between the 75th infantry brigade under the command of *Generalmajor* von Boeckmann and the Russian troops of the 15th corps under the command of general Martos, consisting of the 6th and 8th infantry division. Supporting *Landwehr* units fled for the heavy Russian artillery firing. A crisis was imminent. The Russian infantry took advantage of the panic on the German side by moving forward to the southern outskirts of Frankenau. The German artillery arrived just in time to bring the assault to a halt. Next the Russians started an infantry attack on both sides of the road between Rontzken and Frankenau. The brigade managed to beat them off and Von Boeckmann reported that the positions of both sides were barely 400 to 600 metres separated from one another.

The situation of the 73rd infantry brigade at Lahna was even more serious. First of all the Russians had reconnoitred the road by sending three Cossacks in the direction of Lahna. As soon as they were spotted by German artillery they opened fire and the Russian units disintegrated. This was followed by a large-scale infantry assault from Dietrichsdorf in the direction of Lahna – Allendorf. When also a hill west of town threatened to fall into Russian hands, it turned out that this part of the 37th division was getting surrounded. The Germans had to withdraw over the Alle at Orlau and set the bridge on fire. The Russians followed at close length suffering heavy losses as a result of German firing. When subsequently the attack focused on the 73rd brigade again, Von Staab was forced to send reinforcements, including the 151st infantry regiment. In total four and a half German battalions charged at the Russians. Terrible fights followed. Major Schelle, commander of the second battalion of the regiment (II/151) was killed while leading his men, holding his sword. Major Hupfeld, commander of I/151, was seriously injured. Jaeger-commander Weigelt was killed during the attack of the bridge at Orlau. The commander of the 73rd brigade, Wilhelmi, was forced to intervene personally. He popped up between his men, riding his grey, as if he was on the parade ground. Members of his staff, carrying their rifle, were close behind him. Towards the afternoon the marshy area near the Alle was back in German hands, but many soldiers were standing up to their knees in the mud. Staabs now brought in a last battalion (III/46) led by commander Von Heydebreck, also on horseback; they threw the Russians even further back along the road from Allendorf to Orlau. A Russian banner showing the Saint Andrew's cross was taken from the lifeless body of a Russian officer.

The initial danger seemed to be over for Von Scholz. But a danger corresponding to the one of Gumbinnen now turned up. The German soldiers, like the Russians, were much too eager when they were successful. Von Scholz of the 20th corps had given clear orders not to pursue the Russians on the other shore. Still it happened here and there. That led to confusing fights in the dark. *Generalmajor* Wilhelmi inspected the lines and couldn't help noticing that the various units were running around all over. He tried to restore order and authority and set limited objectives, also because there was heavy fighting going on around Lahna and it wasn't clear yet which side was the strongest. Many of the German officers in the town had been killed.

During the night Von Scholz got into contact with Staabs. He assured Von Stolz that his unit would stand firm on the 24th of August as well, if necessary. That was a great relief for Von Scholz, who after all had received explicit orders from Ludendorff and Von Hindenburg to bring Samsonov to a halt. The defenders tried to utilise the night to their advantage by reuniting the units and bringing them back to their points of departure. The situation wasn't disastrous but far from promising. Wounded men were left behind and complete units were missing. The 11/47 had only two companies left and one company, the 6th, had lost 150 men, including their commander twice. Towards the morning it became clear that the Russians had given up Lahna and Orlau for the time being.

The front was recaptured in some places. Not all units had been informed in time. The next day it became clear that II/50 was still in its position. The Russian quickly slipped past them on both sides. It turned out to be a bloodbath, without any further consequences for the outcome of the battle. The artillery of the German unit was trampled. The gunners defended themselves with shovels and sticks to the last man in bitter hand-to-hand fights.

The next day, August 24, Von Hindenburg and Ludendorff were at Von Scholz headquarters in Muehlen (it was later on moved to Tannenberg). They had made it through the night but reports mentioning new issues started to come in. The Russian 13th corps turned up at Schwedrich, the 14th corps remained active at Orlau – Lahna - Frankenau while south of the German 37th division, near Gilgenburg, the 41st division and the Unger division felt the increasing pressure of the Russian 1st army corps. Furthermore Samsonov brought another corps to the front, the 23rd that had to operate between the 15th and the 1st. Ludendorff and Von Hindenburg understood that the 20th corps was still in great danger. It was extremely important that it wouldn't come to a full-blown showdown since this would, considering the current balance of power, boil down to the complete destruction of Von Scholz forces. Von Scholz therefore received permission to withdraw the central front, near the 37th and 41st infantry division, a little bit, back to the line Damerau - Muehlen. This retreat went well A Russian cavalry division tried to get in between quickly, but was successfully punished for this attempt. Infatuated horses without a rider were running around in front of the German positions.

With this Ludendorff had accomplished his first objective for the *Entscheidungsschlacht*: stabilisation of the front directly opposite the 20th corps. This phase of the battle at Tannenberg has been forgotten by almost everybody by now, but still thousands of men had lost their lives. One brigade alone, part of the 6th Russian infantry division, lost 2,900 men. Total Russian losses during these two days were estimated at around 4,000 men. The Germans took more than 100 prisoners, a small omen of what was to come. General Martos reported to Samsonov that his units were exhausted and asked for a day of rest on the 25th of August. The German front could for a moment heave a sigh of relief, although 1,500 German soldiers had been killed during this prelude to Tannenberg.

During the night of the 24th and the 25th Ludendorff and Hindenburg were gathered around their maps again at their headquarters in Riesenburg. 'So far so good', was the summary of the battle until now, but a number of difficult problems were looming.

Was the front line of Von Scholz strong enough to stand up to Samsonov's assault the next day? Was it possible to bring in additional reinforcements from the Weichsel front to strengthen Von Scholz? Reports had come in about Russian cavalry units that created unrest between Thorn and Mlawa. Were the units marching from north to south on schedule and would it be possible to start their highly necessary attack on the 26th of August? Not only as part of the *Entscheidungsschlacht*, but also as a necessary relieve of the 20th corps of Von Scholz. When were the units of Von Francois ready for action? To what extent were the Russians aware of the fact that the front line of

Von Rennenkampf's Njemen army was completely open? Ludendorff and Von Hindenburg had a few things less to worry about. The objective of Von Scholz corps was clear: to stand firm against Samsonov. 'Any further retreat will mean defeat', Ludendorff said. During a telephone conversation Ludendorff told Von Scholz to 'stand firm until the last man'. It was clear they were playing with fire. Samsonov had 96 battalions at his disposal, the Germans 63, which were partly made up out of *Landwehr*-units. These calculations of Ludendorff and Von Hindenburg were based on the assumption that the Russian forces consisted of the 1st, 13th and 15th corps, while new units were already turning up. But there was no alternative.

The situation looked a little bit more positive with the units that were approaching to Allenstein. Everything was going according to plan and even an opportunity arose here. One of Samsonov's units, the 23rd corps, had fanned out in the direction of the approaching units of Von Below and Von Mackensen and offered a chance of a lifetime. Disturbing news on the other hand was received from the area of Von Rennenkampf's army, which had come into motion again. The question arose whether Ludendorff and Von Hindenburg really would be able to use the troops of Von Below and Von Mackensen for their *Entscheidungsschlacht* or whether they were required north of the Masurian Lakes. Finally there were the forces of Von Francois, whereby Von Hindenburg urged him to start the assault on the 26th from the southwest, as part of the *Entscheidungsschlacht* and also to relieve Von Scholz. It was clear that the cards hadn't been shuffled yet at that moment and the outcome of the battle at Tannenberg was still undecided.

But in the hours that followed things took a turn. The German OHL got hold of two Russian orders, shortly one after another, which had been sent disorderly and hadn't been encoded. The first one concerned the Njemen army of Von Rennenkampf. It contained the targets of their advance: Gerdauen – Allenburg – Wehlau. Ludendorff uttered a sigh of relieve. This wasn't far into Prussian territory. It was clear that the Russians, also because of re-supply problems, didn't operate very fast. The units of Von Below, Von Mackensen and Von Francois had rightfully been released for the *Entscheidungsschlacht*. Shortly afterwards the second order, sent by radio and intercepted by the radio station at Thorn, fell into German hands. It gave valuable information on Samsonov's Narew army. Also here the targets were set so limited that Ludendorff understood it wouldn't come to a decisive battle with the 20th corps of Von Scholz. This would allow him to maintain his front line and make it furthermore possible to slowly start with closing in on the Russians from both the south and the north on the 26th of August. The most important conclusion that could be drawn from these intercepted messages was that both Von Rennenkampf and Samsonov had no idea of the German regroupings and the operation against the Narew army that was getting closer.

In the course of the 25th of August Ludendorff's situation became more relaxed. The signs were favourable, although they were still in danger. A military reconnaissance aircraft had detected many Russian trains, which were bringing reinforcements from Warsaw to the front. This was alarming news, but Ludendorff rightly calculated

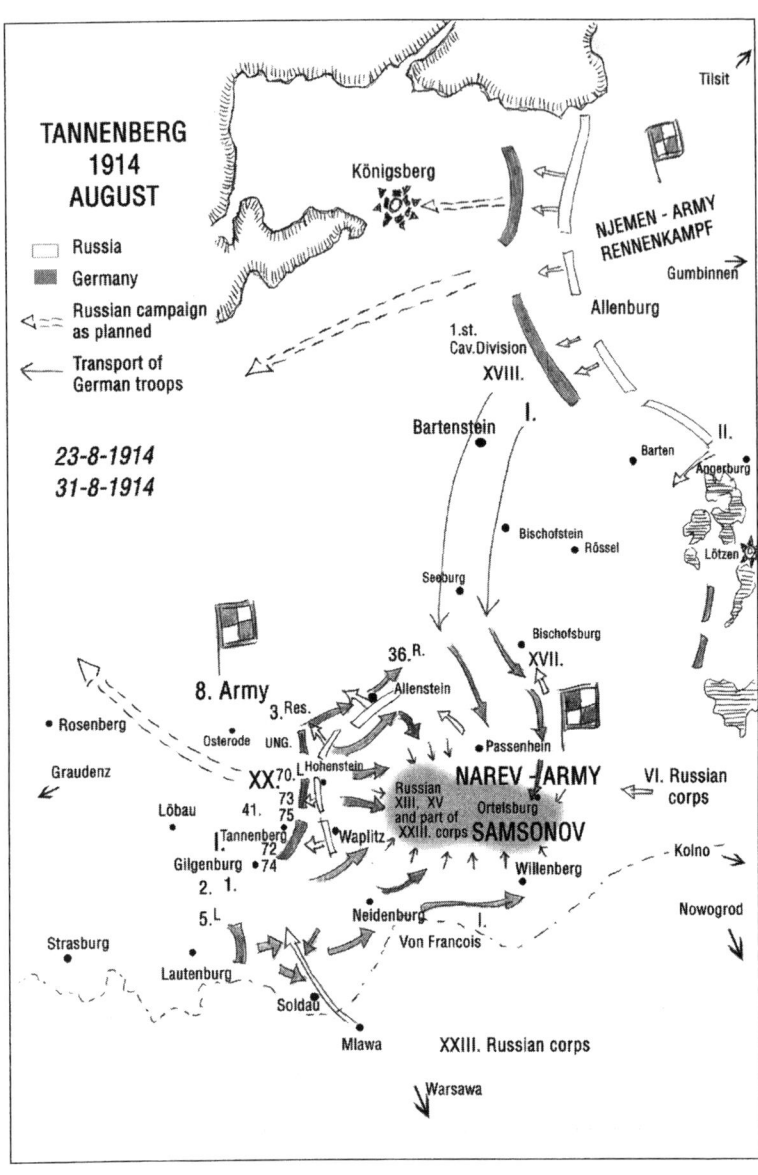

Tannenberg August 1914.

that these wouldn't be in time for the decisive battle he had planned for the 26th of August. He would need a couple of more days to round it off, all in all enough time to stay ahead of the Russian reserves.

On the 25th of August the 17th corps and the 1st reserve corps of Von below and Von Mackensen reached the area between Gr. Schwansfeld and Seeburg. The 6th *Landwehr*-brigade from Lötzen joined them just southwest of Roessel. The 20th corps of Von Scholz remained in their positions around Hohenstein – Muehlen – Tannenberg and got on their southern flank, around Gilgenberg and Lautenburg, support from the units of the combative Von Francois and his 1st corps. Because of all this good news Ludendorff and Von Hindenburg dropped their last 'but'. Up till then Von Mackensen had directed two units towards the south slowly, in order to be able to hit Von Rennenkampf in his southern flank in case this would become necessary. While time passed by slowly on the 25th, Ludendorff and Von Hindenburg decided this was the right moment. 'Everybody towards the south', was the order Von Mackensen received. Not one soldier, except the 1st cavalry division, was now located between the Masurian Lakes and the fortress of Königsberg. A humble division defended a front line of 50 kilometres, but Von Rennenkampf operated very carefully. We attack on the 26th, was Ludendorff's opinion. To be of immediate use to the battered 20th corps, Von Francois had to begin an attack in the direction of Usdau, located along the road Marienburg – Warsaw. For this purpose his corps, with its 1st and 2nd infantry brigade on the south flank near Zielun just across the Russian border, would get support from the 5th *Landwehr*-brigade, an unit consisting of 6 battalions, supported by an squadron and 22 pieces of artillery, under the command of *Generalleutnant* von Muelmann.

But about this plan in particular, Ludendorff had to fight his 'biggest battle' on the 25th of August, namely with the notorious troublemaker Von Francois. Von Francois, whose troops were slowly trickling in, met with Ludendorff in the afternoon and informed him determinedly that encirclement seemed a much better option to him than the break-through that Ludendorff had in mind. Von Francois wanted to move around the 1st Russian corps of the Narew army, via Zielun, where the *Landwehr* was located, via Lopowjez to Mlawa and from here attack Samsonov in his southern flank. But Ludendorff wasn't Von Prittwitz and immediately opposed this plan fiercely. An encirclement manoeuvre of the 1st corps would take a lot of time again and Ludendorff didn't want to lose any more of it. He wanted to support the 20th corps, besides the attack of Von Francois had been coordinated with the 17th corps and the 1st reserve corps and he wanted to stick to his 'stage-agreement'. The plan of Von Francois would also imply an extension of the front and the 8th army didn't have enough units for that. There ought to be moderation in everything, and in this case Ludendorff was right. The 1st corps of Von Francois and the units of the *Landwehr* that had been assigned to him had to attack in the direction of Usdau, roll up the Russian 1st corps under the command of general Artamanow and his chief of staff Blagoheschtschenski (22nd and 24th infantry division) and as a result of this separate them from the rest of Samsonov's army. This way Von Francois would also become a real threat to the southern flank of the Narew army. It became a tough discussion. The historian Wolfgang Venohr characterised Von Francois as 'from top to toe a Prussian, a man as hard as steel, without any respect for his superiors if he thought he was right'. But Ludendorff had been cast in the same mould and didn't give an inch in this first command-conflict since he had arrived in Prussia. 'I'm not used getting my orders from younger officers' Von Francois snapped at Ludendorff. 'You'll better get used to it then' Ludendorff answered with angrily pursed lips. 'The conversation became boisterous', H. Rewaldt wrote in his book *Tannenberg*. It was Von Hindenburg who finally intervened, after having listened silently at first. '*Die Wucht seiner Dienstjahre zwang Von Francois zum nachgeben*'. Convinced they had their way both left the headquarters of Von Francois.

Wolfgang Venohr called this decision on the 25th of August, a limited break-through at Usdau, decisive for the battle at Tannenberg. This raises too much the impression that Ludendorff made a sudden decision on the afternoon of the 25th or that something unique and exceptional had happened. This wasn't the case. It was indeed a typical Ludendorff decision, to move the operation forward by means of a relatively small tactical move and to dismiss a bigger, more ambitious plan with strategic consequences. It was the interplay of forces between strategy and tactics. The strategy, the *Entscheidungsschlacht*, had only roughly been outlined by Ludendorff, whereby he let the weight of the *Entscheidung (decision)* depend, until late into the day of the 25th, on the movements of Von Rennenkampf, after which he released the last units of Von Mackensen. After that he completed the operation taking one step at a time, always willing to make corrections if necessary. Here Ludendorff made the right decision, however in the spring of 1918 these tactics meant his downfall.

After these long and tense days the 26th of August finally dawned. At last Ludendorff could place his counter-attack. The orders were given. The 1st corps of Von Francois had to attack in the direction of Usdau and would be supported by the right (southern) wing of the 20th corps. The remainder of the front of Von Scholz had to stay defensive, only near Hohenstein, on the northern flank, the 3rd reserve division had to be brought to the front. On the 26th of August the front of the 20th and 1st corps looked like this from north to south: the 3rd reserve division at Eichenau, the Unger division at Poeltzdorf, the 37th division at Tannenberg, the 41st division at Gilgenburg, the 1st division at Tautschken, the 2nd division at Kielpinj and the 5th 'Landwehr' at Lautenburg. On the other side were located, also from north to south, the Russian 13th, 15th and 23rd corps, around 9 divisions in total, plus two division, the 3rd guard and the 1st, on its way via Mlawa.

But Ludendorff was disappointed in his high expectations and again it was Von Francois who was the pivot of everything. Von Francois had, during the night of the 25th and the 26th, carefully observed that a large part of the artillery corps still hadn't arrived. The attack was nevertheless planned for the next day. The two divisions of Von Francois and the supporting *Landwehr* did indeed get into action. The troops crossed the river Welle, while pioneers of the corps attempted to build another bridge. The first target of Von Francois was the town of Steeben, but the conditions of the terrain were in favour of the defending Russians. The crossing of the river by the 1st division of general Von Conta went according to plan, but on the eastern bank near Seeben the German units, the 41st infantry regiment and the 2nd infantry brigade of *Generalmajor* von Paschen, came under Russian (artillery) fire. Von Francois moved his own headquarters to the east bank of the Welle quite soon and reviewed the situation at Tautschken in person. With Gumbinnen still in mind the commander of the 1st corps decided that it would be irresponsible to continue the attack on Seeben without sufficient artillery support. It is true that new batteries arrived continuously but their deployment would take time. Von Francois decided to stop with the attack of the 1st division! The situation with the 2nd division wasn't much better. Under the command of *Generalleutnant* von Falk the unit managed to conquer the town of Gr. Koschlau after the Russian army had evacuated it. The attack started slowly because of the swampy terrain, additionally the Russians fired at the German troops with their artillery from the direction of Usdau, the actual target of Von Francois. The 5th *Landwehr*-brigade under the command of *Generalleutnant* von Muelmann hardly fired a shot on the 26th of August. At any chance of a serious confrontation, the Russian pulled back and effectively disturbed the German advance with snipers and artillery.

Ludendorff and Von Hindenburg were desperate. 'I was deeply disappointed' Ludendorff admitted 'when the conquest of Usdau didn't take place. The fact that the attack of Von Francois came to a halt had its consequences, as the assault of 20th corps depended on the advance of the 1st corps. This long awaited day therefore started with a setback. Von Francois nevertheless stuck to the opinion that a true break-through could only take place when his 112 cannons had arrived. Von Francois agreed to meet his commanders insofar that his troops did whatever they could and in any case had won some ground. The German railroads also did their best. This led to unusual images of modern warfare. A German train with an infantry battalion on board even rode as far as the railroad bridge at Tautschken, while the Russian artillery grenades struck everywhere around the train. The battalion was unloaded under fire and directed straight to the front. There wasn't even time for a meal from the field kitchen. 'The troops walked in the direction of the artillery fire with a grumbling stomach', the *Reichsarchiv* wrote.

As a result of this setback with the corps of Von Francois, the front of the 20th corps was also partly condemned to remain passive. After all it was the objective of Von Scholz to carry out a supportive attack, but without a true offensive of Von Francois there wasn't that much to support. The artillery duel between both armies did continue however. This led to the strange situation that the German artillery officer Hell had to fire on his hometown Gutshof, because it was occupied by the Russians; a painful situation. When it became clear around 1.00 pm that Von Francois had made a start with his assault and Ludendorff had sent *Oberquartiermeister* Gruenert to Von Scholz to urge him into action, the corps finally attacked at 2.45 pm.

That still had quite a relative meaning within the 20th corps. Proportionally the Russians were the strongest here. A problem occurred with the 37th infantry division at Muehlen, because of the fact that the Russians had strongly entrenched themselves in the hills and the Russian artillery operated very effectively. A Russian general of the artillery, who had been captured, noticed that he had never seen such effective Russian artillery fire as at

Muehlen, not even during his campaigns in Manchuria. Indeed most of the town went up in flames and had to be partly evacuated by the German troops. Here and there some ground was won during counterattacks. It turned out that the German infantry still had a good morale and it advanced with a loud 'Hurrah'.

The 41st division, the only unit without front line experience, achieved better results. The men had been forced to retreat for days and all energy came out now. 'Our boys are on the loose', the *Reichsarchiv* reported. The infantry lined up at Gilgenburg, across wide potato fields. The Germans effectively fought the Russian artillery and their infantry had to retreat. At 5.45 pm the 152nd regiment entered Ganshorn, 200 Russian soldiers had been taken prisoner. The Germans lost 9 officers and 63 men. Other units were less fortunate: the 148th regiment lost 600 men and with the 72nd infantry brigade 550 persons were killed, wounded or missing.

The 27th, a day later than planned, had to give the final break-through. Von Hindenburg and Ludendorff were already early on their way to personally take care of the coordination of the 1st and 20th corps. For this reason the headquarters of the 8th army had been transferred from Riesenburg to Loebau. The day started like a dream. Very early the report came in that Usdau had been conquered by the troops of Von Francois. 'The battle has been won!' the very tense Ludendorff exclaimed. But the joy didn't last long. It turned out to be false. When Ludendorff and Von Hindenburg arrived in Gross Damerau, they heard the town was under German artillery fire but hadn't been taken yet. In the town and the hills around it the Russian units persistently stood firm. It was of the utmost importance that Von Francois would now break trough in order to begin with the encirclement from the south and to relieve Von Scholz. Units of the 1st division of Von Conta now lined up frontally towards Usdau, while other units, including regiment *Kronprinz* (crown prince), made an enveloping movement from the north. Around noon the German units entered the town from three sides. Two hundred Russians of the 85th infantry regiment who had defended the town until the last moment were taken prisoner. Usdau had fallen!

The old war-horse Von Francois had kept his word. After the arrival of his cannons he had struck, and with success. He personally rode along the positions and saw the hills, strewn with fallen Russians. 'It was one of the most horrible images I ever saw'. From there he rode on to Usdau where Von Conta had already arrived at 11.30 am. Von Francois now smelled blood, started the pursuit and rode on to Niostoy. The Russians fell back into the direction of

Soldau – Mlawa. It was estimated that the Russian 1st corps of general Artamanow lost 2,000 and the Germans around 430 men.

The assignments of the 20th corps were also on the 27th of August quite limited. They had to stand firm and pressurize. Of greater importance was the victory of Von Francois and what happened on the northern flank, with Von Below and Von Mackensen. The *Entscheidungsschlacht* went promising here. Some of the units had a march of over 200 kilometres behind them. Their biggest enemy so far had been pace; many units had a lot of *Fusskranke*, soldiers with foot problems, as a result of which many units were thinned out. Some of the horseman units had ridden so much that the horses had to be guided by hand. On the 26th the corps of Von Mackensen had arrived with the 35th and 36th division east of the Grosslautersee. The 1st reserve corps attacked the Russian positions south of this lake, just west of Gr. Boessauersee, near Klein Boessau and Sauerbaum. A break-through followed on both fronts, which meant that Von Below and Von Mackensen met each other near Gross Boessau and Kleinsack, north of Bischofsburg. From there the units march on to Passenheim on the 27th. Near Mensguth they caught up with a Russian supplies column and got hold of 200,000 rouble of military pay. It was clear that the Russian 6th corps was completely surprised by the attack from the north. Samsonov's advance had suddenly altered into a retreat, during which more and more units, including artillery, were trampled. Ludendorff ordered his troops to get as closely to Allenstein as they could that day, something several units actually managed.

On the 28th Ludendorff and Von Hindenburg went to the headquarters of Von Scholz, just south of Gilgenburg. Each time Ludendorff decided to visit the sector of the front that suffered the most problems. Now that the attack from the south (Von Francois) and the north (Von Below, Von Mackensen) went so well it was important to also pull the front of the 20th corps loose. But this turned out to be harder than expected. The front was still under heavy pressure from the Russian 15th and 23rd corps, whereby especially the 15th caused a lot of problems between Reichenau and Muehlen. Consultation made it clear that an offensive was out of the question, even worse, regroupings would have to take place in order to prevent a Russian break-through. The 37th division was moved from the front near Tannenberg to the north flank of the 20th corps and a new *Landwehr*-unit, Goltz, was quickly brought in. 'We returned dissatisfied' Ludendorff said looking back on his visit to Von Scholz. Although it was very disappointing that Von Scholz couldn't start with his offensive and even had to bring every man into action to counterbalance Samsonov's forces, there was a positive aspect to all this. Because Samsonov was still marching in western direction it became evident that the Russians still hadn't figured out what was happening: the encirclement of the Russian centre, while the 6th corps on the north flank and the 1st on the south flank were being pushed back. It left the 23rd, 15th and 13th corps in the middle: the units that had to be crushed in the *Entscheidungsschlacht*.

Ludendorff's first targets were the Russian 13th and 15th corps. The 1st corps of Von Below was ordered to approach them in their back, while Von Mackensen had to protect the east flank in the direction of Ortelsburg and Jedwabno. But also here Ludendorff had to stay on top of everything in order to make corrections. Major Drechsel of the 1st corps reported that the Russians at Allenstein put up a good fight. Based on this information Ludendorff decided to deploy the entire Goltz division on the most northern flank of the 20th corps. The unit was brought to Biessellen by train and from there they advanced to an area just north of Hohenstein. This meant that the Russian 12th and 15th corps had been separated from each other, even if it was only by the *Landwehr*.

Then another alarming report comes in. The Russian corps on the north flank, the 13th, was retreating from the area around Allemstein to Hohenstein, exactly in the rear of the *Landwehr* that had just arrived. Ludendorff ran the risk this tactical advantage would slip away from him. There is no way back, in spite of all these problems the 20th corps has to fully focus on it. The regrouping of the 37th infantry division to the north flank is completed noticeably quickly and almost immediately the unit is put into action at Reichenau. Also the 3rd division advances in eastern direction. The 41st division, on the south flank of the 20th corps, has to turn north now in order to become a major burden to the Russian 15th corps. This operation, an advance to Paulsgut via Waplitz, was difficult, an emergency measure. The division of *Generalmajor* Sonntag had to pay a high price for it. Despite support from the cavalry of Lewinski and 'König Albert von Saksen', brave dragoons from Allenstein, the units marched straight into the firing of the Russian 8th and 2nd infantry. It is true that these units are also disconcerted, but the forced character of the offensive made the German attack even more costly. The developments with the 41st division were described in detail by *Oberstleutnant a.D.* (a.D.= retired) Albert Benary' in 1933. Sonntag had given his orders for the attack in the early hours of the morning. The 4th Posener regiment nr. 59 'Freiherr Hiller von Gaertringen' had been gathered for that purpose. The morning fog was 'as thick as potato soup' Benary wrote, the soldiers couldn't see anything. Without a compass one was helplessly lost. The Russian troops, especially the 2nd Russian infantry division, were fully prepared and waiting in ambush. The regiment was soon in major trouble. Consequently general Sonntag ordered to relieve the regiment nr. 59. But this attack also failed because of heavy Russian machine gun fire. The units retreated quickly to their preceding positions near Seythen. The advance to Waplitz across the heath of Adam had become a costly adventure. According to Benary the majority of the regiment nr. 59 had been destroyed. This is slightly exaggerated, but their losses were considerable. On the 28th the division lost around 1300 men and 28 officers. The Russian losses are not known. 159 men were buried near Waplitz later on.

Among the losses on German side were over 300 men under the command of major Zickhardt who had been taken prisoner in Waplitz. They got cut off from the rest of their division and had run out off ammunition. An attempt to breakout, according to Benary while singing *Deutschland über alles*, was brought to a standstill by heavy Russian fire after only a couple of metres. Major Zickhardt answered by breaking his sword, made his soldiers destroy their weapons and surrendered. The Russians treated their prisoners well. The men of the 41st infantry division were rescued a few days later by their own forces.

But the assault of the 41st division hadn't been for nothing. The quickly arrived 37th division under the command of Von Morgen, with under her command the Unger division, was immediately brought into action against Hohenstein and with success. Russian losses were increasing slowly, in Lichteinen 500 Russians were taken prisoner, in Droebnitz hundreds of Russians were killed in their trenches and near Sauden a Russian column was attacked by surprise by advancing German forces, during which 600 tsarist soldiers got killed. At the end of the day units of the 75th Unger brigade entered the burning town of Hohenstein. A landmark had been reached, although a high price had to be paid on that 28th of August.

But the fall of Hohenstein was not the only success.

Von Francois also accomplished great results. That day the 1st corps marched from the area of Neidenburg to Schmettau and even as far as Willenberg. At the same time the units of Von Mackensen advanced those of Von Francois from the north, through Ortelsburg in the direction of Willenberg. While there were heavy fights near Hohenstein with the Russian 13th and 15th corps, all of them had now been cut off from their hinterland.

These results had to open Samsonov's eyes and they did! Suddenly it had became clear that the centre of the Russian forces were caught in a threatening pincer movement while the front line of Von Below and Von Scholz was located west of them. There was only one way, backwards, while it was still possible. Large parts of the Russian 13th and 15th corps that all of a sudden tried to withdraw, were located around the heavily contested town of Hohenstein. On the 29th Von Below rushed forward and personally took charge of the attack of the 1st reserve division from hill 191, just north of Hohenstein. The units were located in a favourable position to open fire on the retreat route Hohenstein – Morken and the area east of it. Artillery targets were passed on from a balloon and they had to be quite careful not to mix up their own units with those of the Russians. The *Reichsarhciv* reported that it was a shooting match that would hardly occur again during World War One. Infantry, artillery, horses and wagons, everything suddenly seemed to get into motion and offered grateful targets for the German artillery. Somewhere else two battalions of Von Below's reserves seized the pride of two complete Russian divisions. Now the problem was how to convert this catch. They would have to safeguard it, but that would take time and the men of the 1st reserve corps were very tired after the exhausting fights of the last few days. To be absolutely safe the German commander decided to throw all Russian grenades and ammunition into a local lake. A divisional order of that day said: 'The enemy has been completely beaten, we now need to make the most of our success'. The slaughter continued between Waplitz and Kurken. The units of Von Scholz and Von Below shook hands. In different places large groups of Russian soldiers had fallen into German hands. It was all quite disorderly, 500 men here, another 1500 men there. In some locations, mostly wooded areas, it came to rearguard actions with heavy losses. Ludendorff appeared at the front. Meanwhile radio messages of Samsonov had been intercepted. It was clear that the Russians were now aware of the deadly stranglehold of Ludendorff's *Entscheidungsschlacht*. Von Rennenkampf promised support and would urgently send a number of cavalry divisions to the south. It was necessary to strengthen the northern flank of the encirclement and the 37th infantry division received instructions to do so. Because of this, less units were available to destroy Samsonov's central forces, but towards the evening it became clear that these had largely been defeated. In the area of Hohenstein alone the losses on the 29th of August were estimated at 8,000 men. Hohenstein had become a city in flames. 486 German soldiers had been killed. On the hill west of town the Tannenberg memorial would be build.

The advance of Von Francois had almost the characteristics of a *Blitzkrieg*. Russian pilots were taking off in their ramshackle airplanes while the German artillery was firing at the runway. Retreating supply units were caught up by Germans and successfully fired at. Near

Muschaken a cashbox containing 32,000 roubles fell into German hands, plus a large lot of coffee and bread, as well as 600 prisoners. Another 800 men were captured at Willenberg. The catch was collected and taken in western direction by a column of almost 1000 (!) vehicles. Also Von Mackensen's corps kept pace. The *Reichsarchiv* even reported about soldiers that fell asleep during their march, bumped into a colleague and accordingly woke up. They marched on during the night, even though it was very cold. Ortelsburg was in flames when Von Mackensen entered. It had been evacuated by the Russian 6th corps that wasn't part of the encirclement and with two divisions, the 4th and 16th, continued in carrying out rescue attempts. Ortelsburg mad a sad impression. The streets were filled with equipment that was left behind. The population left their shelters in surprise when they heard Germans troops were back in town again. Von Mackensen, like Von Francois, had advanced so quickly that his supply troops hadn't been able to keep up with him. They had to fight on an empty stomach. Von Mackensen ordered his officers to get off their horse and set an example to their men. A strange incident occurred at Jedwabno. While Von Mackensen's artillery fired one shot after another, a Cossack horse with a white flag suddenly approached, straight at the German positions. The unit ceased firing and saw at their surprise that it was major Zickhardt of the German infantry regiment 148 that had fallen into Russian hands earlier. Because of the sudden turnover in the battle, he and more than 400 other soldiers had been released and were now able to join their own forces again!

The bloody conclusion of the battle at Tannenberg occurred on the 30th and 31st of August. They consisted of breakout and rescue attempts of the tsarist army. The breakout attempts included the 13th, 15th and 23rd corps that were roughly located between Burdungen and Omulefofen and tried to escape to the south in the direction of Wallendorf and Rettkowen. But Samsonov's breakout attempt was rather late. West of them the German 3rd reserve division and 41st infantry division were located, south of them the 2nd infantry division and parts of the 1st corps, which together with units from Von Mackensen, the 35th and 36th infantry division, also had cut off the road to the east. A smaller Russian force, which was already located east of the 35th infantry division tried to breakout at Willenberg. The rescue attempts occurred in the east, near Ortelsburg and in the south, near Neidenburg; it involved units of the Russian 6th corps under the command of general Blagovheschtschenski and units of the 1st corps under the command of general Artamanov. Furthermore there was the threat of Von Rennenkampf in the north.

Ludendorff and Von Hindenburg followed the developments tensely. On the evening of the 29th Ludendorff estimated that already 10,000 Russians had been taken prisoner and the 30th brought even more joy. On the battlefield between Allenstein – Hohenstein – Neidenburg and Ortelsburg between 20,000 and 30,000 Russians had been captured. There were also a large number of artillery pieces that had been abandoned in the fields. Von Hindenburg issued a communiqué in which he mentioned that the enemy was beaten and that both the emperor as well as the OHL expressed their appreciation for the dedication of its forces. But there was more good news. It became clear that there wasn't much to fear anymore from Von Rennenkampf's army. Once more Russian radio messages were intercepted. The rescue attempt had been stopped, but it was even better, Von Rennenkampf was retreating! The radio message mentioned that the Russians had to destroy as many rail and telegraph connections as possible during their retreat.

But that didn't mean these days had been without any danger. The most dangerous news during these days came from the south, the attempts to relieve Artamanov! When the reports on this came in via the *Flieger-Abteilung 6* of the fortress Graudenz, units of Von Francois were scattered over a broad front. The only unit that could be brought into action at a right angle to the advance route of the Russian army was a battalion, 1 / 45 of major Schlimm, which was stationed in Neidenburg. Just south of this town, near Berghof, they quickly took their positions. Meanwhile Von Francois started to gather troops from all directions. On Sunday the 30th of August many units of the division took part in the battle at Willenberg. There was not much else to do than to release a number of small units wherever possible and to return immediately to Neidenburg. Von Francois had set up his headquarters in Modlken and from there he attacked the flank of the forces of the Russian 1st corps from an eastern direction. But it would get close. Not much later the report came in that Schlimm could no longer hold the front at Berghof. Von Francois personally galloped to the front of the troops and threw everything available into battle. The encirclement of the majority of Samsonov's forces shouldn't be undone by this relieve attack of Artamanov. Units of the 1st and 2nd infantry division were deployed, artillery units were hastily brought in as well as *Landwehr* units and even units of the 41st infantry division of major general Sonntag, which recently suffered such difficult times, were put into action and with success. The Russian advance started to get stuck as a result of increasing resistance, straight on their marching direction and also on their flank. Artamanov hesitated and subsequently gave up. Around 500 Russian soldiers were taken prisoner at Berghof and 350 were left behind on the battlefield. The *Flieger-Abteilung* of lieutenant Winckler confirmed the retreat of the Russians.

With this retreat the Russians again missed a major opportunity to save Samsonov. In his memoirs Max Hoffmann rightly wonders about the relatively ease with which they managed to hold off Artamanov. It probably was the result of a combination of the energetic appearance of Von Francois, the successful interference of the artillery of Mühlmann, the earlier Russian losses at Usdau and Artamanov's overestimation of the German army. This last explanation was surely an option, because of the fact that Russian intelligence, including their signal service, performed miserably. It appeared that the Russians were more or less operating in the dark and there was hardly any coordination. Hoffmann described the constant flow of not encoded radio messages of the Russians as 'incomprehensible thoughtlessness'.

Another dangerous moment occurred with Von Mackensen. Ortelsburg had already fallen into German hands on the 29th, but general Von Hennig made his men, under the command of major general Von Hahn, directly march on to Wellenberg, more to the south. The small unit that stayed behind in Ortelsburg suddenly turned out to be cut off from their environment by Russian cavalry units of the 6th corps. Von Hahn was in doubt what to do next. On the one hand it was very important for the encirclement to march on to Willenberg. On the other hand it was necessary that the encirclement at Ortelsburg remained intact. The issue was resolved when his units ran into forces of Von Francois that had left Willenberg to meet Von Mackensen. Von Hahn could now order his troops to turn around and successfully rescue Ortelsburg. Heavy fights with the Russians had taken place there. The church tower of the city had collapsed as a result of artillery fire.

The efforts of Von Rennenkampf's Njemen army were these days mainly focused on an advance in western direction, whereby the 1st cavalry division of *Generalleutnant* Brecht continued to slow down the Russian advance as much as possible. In order to give sufficient cover to the forces south of the Masurian Lakes the defence of the north flank had been handed over to the units at Königsberg, under the command of Von Pappritz. This was too heavy a burden for him and he was forced to retreat from the river Alle to defensive positions on the river Deim. Heavy artillery duels evolved at Königsberg. This led to exciting moments on the north flank of the 8th army, but Ludendorff and Von Hindenburg gladly took this for granted as long as it ensured calmness on the southern front. Von Rennenkampf had made an attempt to force the fortress Lötzen, on the road Königsberg – Bjelostok, to surrender but the proud commander Busse described the appeal to surrender, by the Russian negotiator on the 27th of August, as an 'insult' to the defence forces of Lötzen, which consisted of four and a half battalion of *Landwehr* and *Landsturm*, as well as a small artillery unit.

Although they had been lying behind Russian lines since the 25th of August, Busse informed the negotiator that Lötzen would only surrender 'if the garrison had turned into ruins'. The Russians, units of the 2nd army corps of general Scheidemann, happily refrained from an assault. The fortress, safely situated behind a water barricade, wouldn't be easy to take and besides the forces and material had to concentrate on the big catch: Königsberg!

In the shimmering heat of the 31st of August the last Russian breakout attempt, at Puchalowen, was resisted. During one of the last fights the commanding officer of the 1st infantry division, general Von Trotha, had been killed. Near Janowo it had come to heavy fighting with Russian forces from many different units that all tried to escape. The German artillery fired at the enemy lines from close range. Russian priests tried to encourage them. Prayers and singing could be heard among the violence of war. Von Trotha was of the opinion that that a general needed to be in front with his men and personally led his soldiers in their defence. It came to hand-to-hand fights. The Russians, according to Von Francois, again showed their outstanding military attitude by running towards their destruction while singing. Thousands of Russians remained behind, killed. The Russians now started to surrender massively. Cavalry captain Von Puttkamer witnessed a local capitulation of 210 Russian officers and 11,000 men, together with 2,000 horses and 41 pieces of artillery in the neighbourhood of Willenberg. A short meeting with a Russian priest, who had reported himself to the Germans holding a white flag, had preceded the capitulation. More and more generals were now taken prisoner, such as general Klujev of the Russian 13th corps and general Martos of the 15th corps, who had been captured by I / 43 of *Hauptmann* Grun. Von Francois rode along the long lines of prisoners of war, searching for the lifeless body of Von Trotha. He saw the awful sight of a battlefield covered with blood. Here and there, amidst the fallen, lay moaning wounded men. Just in front lay the, during the attack killed, German soldiers of the 12th company of regiment nr. 3. Their hands were still holding their rifle with its bayonet attached. The body of captain Schoene lay in front. Not much further was the big lifeless body of the commander of the Russian 24th infantry regiment. General Von Trotha was found at a forest near Puchlowen. A bullet had pierced his neck. The body was salvaged and placed on the bier in the church of Neidenburg. All officers of battalion regiment nr. 3 had been killed. The units were under the command of their non-commissioned officers. In the middle of the fight, when the troops passed by the lifeless body of one of their commanders, the *Feldwebel* gave orders to march slow and turn their eyes to the right, honouring their fallen commander this way.

IV.

Tannenberg, the aftermath

On the 30th of August a relieved Ludendorff was able to inform Coblenz that already more than 25,000 prisoners of war had been taken away from the battlefield and that this number would quickly increase. This was indeed the case, until the 3rd of September around 92,000 Russians, as estimated by the *Reichsarchiv*, were taken prisoner. Apart from that, thirteen Russian generals, 350 pieces of artillery as well as numerous pieces of equipment and horses had fallen into German hands. The number of Russians that got killed will never be known. 6739 Russians found a resting place in an official grave. The *Reichsarchiv* has estimated the total number of Russians that were killed at 120,000 men. Sixty trains brought the Russian prisoners of war to the hinterland.

German losses were as follows: 1891 killed, 6579 wounded and 4588 missing, a total of 13,058 men. The 20th corps of Von Scholz had the largest number of deceased to mourn for: 631 men. Of those 6579 wounded the 20th corps suffered more than 3,000. It was the price the corps had to pay to prevent a breakthrough of Samsonov to the west. The corps of Von Mackensen, which had suffered such heavy losses at Gumbinnen, was much better off this time, with only 93 killed, 275 wounded and 103 missing, a total of 481 men. After the 20th corps it was Von Francois who had suffered the heaviest losses, 360 killed, 1376 wounded and 597 missing, a total of 2,333 men; but on the other hand he had achieved spectacular results. Furthermore, during the days that followed the number of missing persons became less as wounded men returned to their units, which meant that the total German losses were much smaller than the 13,000 men they anticipated immediately after the battle. The actual losses were determined at 4,000 men, of which the 20th corps with 1417 men and the 1st with 516 men suffered the most.

Immediately after this victory an enormous cheering broke out. The victory, which received the name of the battle at Tannenberg, named after the defeat of the *Ordenritter* who were defeated there by Polish and Lithuanian forces on the 15th of July 1410, had come totally unexpected. Something that was only supposed to win some time Ludendorff and Von Hindenburg had turned into a great victory. The *Entscheidungsschlacht* had become an overwhelming success. Historical comparisons, whether relevant or not, were brought up. Some people compared it with the battle at Sedan during the French-Prussian war of 1870-1871, others with the battle of Cannae in 216 AD when Hannibal with his 40,000 men from Carthage beat 86,000 Roman infantry and cavalry soldiers. The battle plan of Cannae had become Hannibal's military will, an eternal blueprint for encirclement. Weapons had changed, according to Von Francois in his memories of the battle, but tactics and strategy were still the same. Max Hoffmann called the battle 'one of the biggest victories in history'.

But also if we just stick to the facts, Tannenberg was

an extraordinary military event. 153,000 German soldiers had defeated 191,000 Russians, while there was a second large Russian army (Von Rennenkampf) nearby. The situation had changed from an East Prussia under threat into a German counter offensive. The concept of the *Entscheidungsschlacht* had worked, Samsonov's army was more or less beaten and the balance of power on the northern part of the eastern front was now a lot more favourable, although East Prussia wouldn't be safe until also Von Rennenkampf's army had been beaten. With this the scenario for the second fight, the battle at the Masurian Lakes, was born.

While Ludendorff and Von Hindenburg were bent over their maps again for this purpose, the myth of Tannenberg already started to kick up a fuss. This myth not only consisted of distorted historical comparisons but also of forgetting, at least by the overall public, the first lessons at Gumbinnen, during which the tsarist army had proven it was a tough opponent. In brief, the war in the east wasn't over yet. Besides, the eastern front extended beyond Prussia. The developments at the *König und Kaiser* army were much less positive and it wouldn't be long until the German troops would have to operate at this front line like a flying goalie to save it from collapsing. Tannenberg had been an *Entscheidungsschlacht*, not out of luxury but from dire necessity. Ludendorff had chosen for this concept because he understood how alarming the situation was. He rightfully distrusted the northern flank of the Schlieffen Plan and in the middle of the operation Von Moltke had released some of its forces to support the eastern front, which also came from the most distant flank that had to make the biggest turn, although Ludendorff had indicated that he wouldn't need them. They indeed arrived too late for Tannenberg and were absent from a crucial location in the west, although it was hardly imaginable that Schlieffen (Moltke-II) would have been successful if these units had been there, the adjustment to the original Schlieffen Plan had been too radical for that. The *Entscheidungsschlacht* at Tannenberg had therefore mainly been an answer of Ludendorff to his doubts about the actual arrival of large armies in the east after a victory over France. This expectation proved to be realistic. Besides, Tannenberg could also have taken place by an offensive using the inside lines, something in which stage specialist Ludendorff had become an unprecedented specialist as a result of studying the Schlieffen Plan for years, and an actual German offensive towards the east would have other tactical and strategic consequences. At the Masurian Lakes, the battle against Rennenkampf, Ludendorff was still in a position to make use of his inside lines, but the bigger the success, or in other words how further the Germans would operate to the east, the less Ludendorff would be able to exploit his tactical mastery and the more he would need the support of strategic plans, something he really wasn't that good at.

But one of the consequences of Tannenberg was the fact that nobody questioned the actions of the duo Von Hindenburg – Ludendorff anymore. Overnight they had become Germany's heroes. To the outside world it was above all Von Hindenburg's victory, as is shown by the title of the book in which Von Francois wrote down his memories: *Hindenburgs Sieg bei Tannenberg*, in which he also reported the second myth: '*das Cannae des Weltkriegs*', as if the comparison with Hannibal applied (the balances of power alone were completely different) and the race in the east had been run. The Russian army had been defeated but still had millions of soldiers and quite a lot of room at its disposal. But for the average German, *Hochmeister* Ulrich von Jungingen, who was killed at Tannenberg in 1410, had finally been revenged. The historical awareness, and especially the mystification of it, was of very long standing in this part of Europe. It is interesting to realise that the documents published in the days of Tannenberg and the interbellum period point out that the battle of 1410 had been lost from the Lithuanians and Poles because of treason, a kind of early version of the *Dolchstosslegende*, which developed shortly after the collapse in 1918. From a political point of view it wasn't a smart decision to name the battle after Tannenberg as it was humiliating to the Poles. Ludendorff had already pointed out in the past that Berlin hadn't been able to mobilise the Poles sufficiently for the German empire. To the Poles the battle of 1410 symbolised a feat of arms and was known as the battle at Grunwald. Now Tannenberg was shown as the German sword that beat the Slavs on their head, as the historian Karl-Heinz Janssen described it. Other historians from the Ludendorff camp, such as H. Rewaldt, were of the opinion that Tannenberg had not only concerned a fight against the Russians and that the victory was a revenge on an earlier Slav expansion, but that it had also been a battle against 'Rome, Judas and Freemasonry'. The poison of the *Dolchstosslegende* had already penetrated the forbearing paper of the history books by then.

Ludendorff, Von Hindenburg as well as Hoffmann claimed to have come up with the name Tannenberg for the battle. In any case it was Von Hindenburg, as commander, who asked the emperor for his permission, who, because of his political inanity, agreed immediately. Initially Ludendorff had been reserved in making comparisons. Somewhat superstitious as he was the name Tannenberg terrified him, reminded him of a painful historical defeat. According to Karl-Heinz Janssen, Ludendorff refused to set up his headquarters in Tannenberg during the battle. For quite a while the general staff talked about the battle at Allenstein, but in the end it turned this way. Tannenberg became identical to German military success, which brought about a kind of *Marschall vorwärts* mood. It had become a 'symbol of loyalty', loyalty of Germany to the *Deutschtum* in the east. No less than 34,000 Prussian houses had gone up in flames, but German soldiers, willing to sacrifice their life, had stopped the Russian steamroller. 'God gave us a great commander', tell us the documents of those days. Even a new word was invented to honour Von Hindenburg: 'Grossfaz' (*Grösster Feldherr aller Zeiten*, meaning greatest general of all times), forgetting that not Von Hindenburg but Ludendorff had been the man behind Tannenberg. On every order, next to the large signature of Von Hindenburg, was always written the fan-shaped 'L' of Ludendorff. Von Hindenburg had quickly realised that he shouldn't get in the way of the gifted Ludendorff, but had to support him in any way he could. *Ich weiss auch nichts Bessers, Got geb's*, was often his reaction to the proposals of Ludendorff, because Ludendorff was always concrete and always had clear plans, although often focused on the short term they had worked great at Tannenberg.

The shadow of Tannenberg would turn out to be a long one. On the 18th of September 1927, in the presence of Chancellor Marx, a great monument was unveiled near Tannenberg. The designers, the Krueger brothers, architects from Berlin, were in all modesty inspired by Stonehenge. So they went for imperishableness. A year later even a communist representative of the Reichstag expressed his 'highest esteem' for the battle at Tannenberg. Military bases were named after the battle. Tannenberg embraced by military romance, of commanders on hills, waving flags and banners as well as artillery pulled by horses, like in Napoleon's best days. But also these wars had their horrible sides, like the First World War would show the world in an even more extreme way. Tannenberg had also become a *Lehrmodel* of German strategy, while it had much more to do with tactics as a result of a wrong strategy. It was a *Sandkastspiele*, a wrong lesson for the future, part of a dangerous all or nothing scenario, the scenario that had kept Germany firmly in its grip since the Schlieffen Plan.

'If I had lost the battle, only I would have lost it', Von Hindenburg said later on. There was a lot of truth in that remark, because as Tannenberg became more and more an historical fact, also more spiritual fathers of the battle surfaced. Both the vain Ia of the 8th army, Max Hoffmann and Von Francois claimed a large part of the victory later on and Von Francois pointed out that he hade made 60,000 prisoners. No one less than Winston Churchill supported him in this, he gave Von Francois the credits for Tannenberg. It is true that Von Francois had fought bravely and played a major role in the battle, but the whole idea of Tannenberg couldn't be the work of some one who had only operated at corps level. Churchill's opinion was heavily exaggerated. Hoffmann gave a tour of the battlefield later on and showed Von Hindenburg's headquarters with the remark 'this is where the Commander in Chief was sleeping during the battle at Tannenberg'. That didn't make a difference to the public. Tannenberg was always bracketed together with Von Hindenburg, and to a lesser extent with Ludendorff, who would make his claim for the battle after the war and rightfully so. 'Your old man is going to be famous', Von Hindenburg joked in a letter to his wife. And he was right. Of course, Tannenberg, as also mentioned by *Graf* von Kielmansegg and the historian Walter Görlitz, had been the result of many, but as for style and passion as well as bearing the responsibility together with Von Hindenburg, it had been Ludendorff's achievement. Ludendorff has also received these credits in more recent studies, among others things from Wolfgang Venohr, who compared the battle at Tannenberg with two other German tactical victories during the Second World War: Kharkov in March 1943 and Shitomir in November-December 1943, where Paul Haussers 2nd ss corps and Hermann Balcks 48th armoured corps respectively achieved similar victories. This comparison is interesting because these were tactical victories indeed. Tannenberg was only an *Entscheidung* as far as it concerned the fate of Samsonov's army, the war wasn't decided by it.

Samsonov himself didn't experience the end of his army anymore. He was a broken man when the defeat of his troops became clear. He realised the magnitude of his defeat. The numbers only told a part of the story. The forces that the Russian empire had brought into action were first class units, whereas the German opponent was forced to bring in a lot of soldiers from the *Landwehr* and *Landsturm*. All of that made the Russian defeat even more bitterly. 'The tsar trusted me, how can I still face him after such a disaster', Samsonov confided to his subordinates. During his attempts to break out, Samsonov had been troubled by increasing asthma. He fell behind, carrying his map and compass. After he had given a letter for the tsar to some of his soldiers, he withdrew among the trees. A shot was heard. His staff officers immediately knew what this meant. Samsonov had committed suicide. They tried to find his body in the forest, but without any luck. The Russian General Staff remembered that 'no one of the staff officers felt the need to kneel down by the body of Samsonov and to say in farewell 'it wasn't your fault, but ours'. The 'dark' staff officers were in a hurry to continue their escape. The search didn't take long. German signal flares, which illuminated the landscape for a short while, were everywhere. The troops of the German 8th army were on the Russians heels. They moved on in southeast direction and most of the staff officers came through. German troops discovered the lifeless body Samsonov and buried the general at Willenburg. In 1916 his widow, with the help from the Red Cross, managed to bring the body back to Russia where Samsonov was reburied. 'With the dead of Samsonov our hopes also died', said the Russian officer Danilov.

In spite of this tragic event, Russia didn't become aware of the defeat at Tannenberg that quickly. The Russian media also had a lot of good news to report, major successes against the Austrian-Hungarian army in the battle at Lemberg, which would shortly give Ludendorff a lot to worry about. In contrast to the relative public peacefulness regarding Tannenberg in Russia, in Germany a discussion started how this Russian defeat could be explained. What had gone wrong with this, at least on paper, strong Russian army? The rumour went around that there was an old feud between both Russian corps commanders, Von Rennenkampf and Samsonov. It would go all the way back to the battle at Liauyang where Samsonov had to defend the Yantai coalmines at that time. The Siberian Cossacks of Samsonov weren't able to cope with the Japanese forces and he had unsuccessfully requested Von Rennenkampf for help. Both generals had met at the station of Mukden later on and according to the legend their adjutants had to jump in between in order to prevent a fight. But because the tsar only wanted to deploy his best generals in East Prussia, they had been ordered 'to put up with each other'. Before they went to the front the grand duke had arranged a meeting between both men, to clear the sky. Von Rennenkampf and Samsonov had met at Snamenka where they, in the presence of the grand duke Sergey Mikhailovitsch and Shilinski, shook hands. Von Rennenkampf would have been 'visibly touched' by this gesture. He said with an unusual insecure voice: 'At this moment there are no personal hostilities. We should only think of the victory of our armies and of Russia'. The story goes that when they said good-bye, Shilinski shook both general's hands and told them that Liauyung had been forgotten.

Although there are indications of tension between both commanders – Tuchman speaks of the 'strange behaviour of Von Rennenkampf' – is the conclusion that these formed the basis of the German successes exaggerated. Both commanders obeyed their superior officer, so if there was a question of poor communication they were to thank for it. The *Reichsarchiv* assumes there were possible irritations between both commanders, but nothing proves that these have influenced the battle in a negative way. Recent studies, like the one of the British historian John Keegan do not mention anything of tensions. That is strange, because according to Max Hoffmann the rumour that there was some animosity between the Russian commanders circulated already during the days of Tannenberg. In his memoirs Hoffmann wrote that he had discussed it with Ludendorff at that time. Ludendorff was also curious about the Russian operation. He had sent for the Russian general Martos, commander of the Russian 15th corps (6th and 9th infantry division). During his attempt to break out he had run into two Polish farmers who were willing to give him directions. These Poles had lured him straight into a German ambush, which killed his chief of staff, general Machugovsky. Von Francois however treated Martos like a gentleman, invited him into his car and offered him chocolate and wine, as a good host should. Ludendorff asked him what the Russian plans had been and Martos answered that he had only been informed on tactical matters. At that moment, as is written by the Canadian historian Goodspeed, Von Hindenburg walked in. Martos was startled by his tall stature. Von Hindenburg took the right hand of Martos in both his hands and quietly addressed him in lingering Russian. He told him that he had fought bravely and would get his sword back. After that both Ludendorff and Von Hindenburg left the room, aware that they probably would never get a complete understanding of what had happened on Russian side.

What is clear is that the so-called tensions between Von Rennenkampf and Samsonov during the Russo-Japanese war – if they occurred! – were possibly outshined by other problems of a more technical nature, as a result of which true communication between both armies was impossible. This is what Norman Stone mentions in his standard work 'The Eastern Front 1914-1917'. The tension between Von Rennenkampf and Samsonov went back to more or less general tensions within the Russian army, which had been subject to reforms since its defeat in the Russo-Japanese war. Part of the general staff supported the traditionalists, who only wanted a few changes, while others were keen on making a lot of them. The commanders of Von Rennenkampf and Samsonov belonged to different parties and this resulted in poor communication. When Von Rennenkampf made the turn in the direction of Königsberg instead of coming to Samsonov's rescue, he simply followed his orders, as is confirmed by the radio messages that were intercepted by the Germans. This fact makes the existence of a conflict between Samsonov and Von Rennenkampf of minor importance.

Another myth about the Russian defeat would be the fact that the Russians had operated in a hurry, in order to help their French allies. 'France owes the victory at the Marne to the self-sacrifice of Russia', the tsarist Minister of Foreign Affairs, S.D. Sasonoff wrote in his memoirs and added that Samsonov hadn't been ready to invade Prussia. In reality the tsarist army had been heavily rebuild since 1906 and Moscow spent one third of its budget on the military. It is true that a lot of money was spent on prestigious things, such as the Russian fleet that had almost completely been destroyed by Japan, but also emperor Wilhelm II who was just as vain permitted himself this 'luxury'. In 1914 Moscow had more than 114 divisions at its disposal again, compared to 96 German ones. They also had 6,720 pieces of artillery, compared to 6,004 on the German side. The Russian railroads were able to mobilise 100 divisions in just eighteen days, which indicated that Russia's social backlog on the west was a lot bigger than its military. This social backlog was proven by the fact that more than one third of the Russian officers hadn't even completed secondary school and the fact that the majority of their generals weren't ethnic Russians, even worse, seven generals had a German name. Their dependency of 'foreign' commanders didn't always result in a soft treatment of its soldiers. Stone gives the example of an officer who 'learned his lesson' during the Russo-Japanese war whereby he imputed the failure of the Russians to cowardice. In order to punish them he took away their rifles. Now there was no other alternative than to get close to the enemy. In reality this was caused by faulty equipment but that had more or less been resolved by 1914. During the last few years Russia had even spent more money on their military than Germany.

The principal reason for the Russian failure was the poor communication with the Russian high command and between the corpses themselves. This happened partly by letter. There were only a handful of telephone lines available and telegraph equipment was rare as well as slow. Besides, Von Rennenkampf was under the impression that he had achieved an important victory at Gumbinnen and the Germans were retreating. His reconnaissance during the days that followed had failed disastrously. From the orders that Samsonov received from his superiors he had understood that the German army was withdrawing, therefore he hadn't seen the pincer movement coming.

It has been correctly pointed out that the Russian army apparently relied too much on its superiority and underestimated the Germans. The deployment of the Russian forces was dispersed while Ludendorff centralised them. The Germans had another important ally, as Hoffmann expressed later on: the Russians themselves. Because the Germans had been able to intercept their orders they were able to take substantial risks that brought about successes on the battlefield. This resulted in a successful *Entscheidungsschlacht*. While the soldiers were preparing their bivouac and sang the song of thanks *Schlacht of Leuthen*, Von Hindenburg and Ludendorff walked into the church of Allenstein. They attended the service in this old German town of knights. God had been merciful to Germany.

Finally also Ludendorff himself refuted a myth about the Russian army. In various studies it was alleged that thousands of Russians drowned in swamps. This isn't correct, there wasn't a swamp anywhere around, Ludendorff wrote in his memoirs.

V.

Epilogue

Tannenberg; when looking back, this town and battle symbolise an atypical episode during World War One: the war of movement. In reality the war quickly turned into a trench war, like we knew in the west.

With the battle at Tannenberg and the ones that followed, which all ended quite positively for Germany, Ludendorff had left his visiting card. Ultimately this brought the duo Von Hindenburg – Ludendorff to the absolute military top of Germany. As from 1917 they dictated, together with the emperor, the development of the war. Ludendorff left such a heavy mark upon everything, people also referred to it as 'Ludendorff's dictatorship'. He didn't only interfere in military matters, but also in politics, the war economy, propaganda and he played a decisive role in major war decisions in other areas, such as diplomacy and the submarine war. In the end the war identified itself with Ludendorff, who had to make room when the unavoidable defeat got there in 1918.

This was a bitter disappointment for Ludendorff. He never got over it and it was the beginning of his alienation from imperial Germany in which he had grown up and the start of his political career that was quickly marked by the *Dolchstosslegende*. His role in the early Hitler movement and his participation in the Hitler-Putsch in 1923 have coloured the view on Ludendorff's character. Because of this we have lost touch with the curious history of Tannenberg and the battles that followed until the winter of 1915, which were of a major historical significance. These battles haven't been decisive. They didn't bring victory to Germany. The victory at Tannenberg however did save East Prussia from a Russian invasion in 1914. When at the end of the Second World War the Red Army approached the memorial in remembrance of the battle, German engineers blew it up.

In this short monograph I have tried to reflect the history of the battle at Tannenberg. More than 65 years after Ludendorff passed away and almost 90 years after the battle, it will help us to remember the difficult genesis of the Europe we know now.

Erich Ludendorff (on the right) and Paul von Hindenburg, a painting by Hugo Vogel.

Paul von Hindenburg was older than Erich Ludendorff and already retired when the war broke out in 1914. The German High Command reappointed him. This picture shows Von Hindenburg at a much younger age, in July 1871.

The concerns of the German borderland shown in a theatrical way. Von Hindenburg is witnessing the flight of German civilians.

Ludendorff understood the dangerous situation for Prussia. This picture shows his birthplace in Kruschevina near Posen.

Mobilisation of the troops. There were no clear plans for the fight in the east.

Erich Ludendorff, second in command, but the brains behind the German actions.

Erich Ludendorff and his second wife Dr Mathilde von Kemnitz. Because of her radical world vision, Ludendorff alienated from his supporters after the First World War.

Barbwire fences near the Lötzen fortress.

Russian civilians on the run.

The self-willed general Von Francois.

Otto von Below.

Von Mackensen.

The Russian general Samsonov.

The town of Marienburg

Von Hindenburg and Ludendorff made a successful team.

Their influence on emperor Wilhelm II quickly increased after the battle at Tannenberg.

A major victory is taking shape on the map.

Russian prisoners of war near Tannenberg.

A major monument was raised at Tannenberg.

A memorial at Tannenberg.

Ortelsburg, 1914.

The Russian general Markos in captivity.

The generals Von Morgen and Von Francois.

Seized Russian positions near Usdau.

Russian prisoners of war.

The battle at Tannenberg was commemorated every year.

Paul von Hindenburg became a national hero in Germany after the battle at Tannenberg, but Ludendorff was the spiritual father behind most operations.

Von Hindenburg and Ludendorff, both present at one of the annual commemorations.

Bibliography

Andriessen, J.H.J., *De andere waarheid. Een nieuwe visie op het ontstaan van de Eerste Wereldoorlog 1914-1918* (1999)

Baer, C.H., *Der Völkerkrieg. Eine Chronik der Ereignisse seit dem 1.Juli 1914* (Stuttgart)

Benary, A., *Die Schlacht bei Tannenberg* (Leipzig 1933)

Bircher, E./Bode, W., *Schlieffen. Mann und Idee* (Zurich 1937)

Bruce, A., *An illustrated Companion to the First World War* (London 1989)

Buetow, W.J., *Hindenburg, Heerführer und Ersatzkaiser* (Bergisch Gladbach 1984)

Czech-Jochberg, E., *Die Verantwortlichen im Weltkrieg* (Leipzig 1932)

Dittrich, Z.R., *De opkomst van het moderne Duitsland. Dromen, worstelingen. Tegenslagen 1806-1862* (Groningen/Djakarta 1956)

Falkenhayn, E. von, *Die Oberste Heeresleitung 1914-1916 in ihren wichtigsten Entschliessungen* (Berlin 1920)

Von Francois, *Hindenburgs Sieg bei Tannenberg. Das Cannae des Weltkrieges in Bild und Wort* (Leipzig 1923)

Frenz, H., *Hindenburg und Ludendorff und ihr Weg durch das Deutsche Schicksal* (Berlin 1937)

Freund, M., *Deutsche Geschichte von den Anfaengen bis zur Gegenwart* [1975] (1981)

Generalstabes des Feldheeres (hg.)., *Der grosse Krieg in Einzeldarstellungen.* Heft 20 Die Winterschlacht in Masuren. Unter Benützung amtlichen Materials bearbeitet von Von Redern, Hauptmann der reserve damals Kompagnie-Führer im Infanterie-Regiment Graf Barfuss (4.Westfäl.) Nr.17 (Oldenburg 1918)

Goodspeed, D.J., *Ludendorff* [London 1966] (Hier gebruikt: Ludendorff. Soldat, Diktator, Revolutionär (1966)

(Der) Grosse Krieg. Eine Chronik von Tag zu Tag. Urkunden, Depeschen und Berichte der Frankfurter Zeitung (1914)

Hindenburg,Von, *Aus meinem Leben* (Leipzig 1927)

Hoffmann, M., *Der Krieg der versäumten Gelegenheiten* (München 1923)

Hoffmann, M., *Tannenberg wie es wirklich war* (Berlin 1926)

Jackel,E., *Das Deutsche Jahrhundert* (Stuttgart 1996)

Kybitz,W., *Ludendorffs Handstreich auf Lüttich* (München 1939)

Ludendorff, E., *Meine Kriegserinnerungen 1914-1918.* 6e druk. (Berlin 1920)

Liddell Hart, B., *History of the First World War* [1970] (London 1973)

Lindenberg,P., (hg.), *Hindenburg Denkmal für das Deutsche Volk.* (Berlin 1925)

Ludendorff, E., *Mein militärischer Werdegang. Blätter der Erinnerung an unser stolzes Heer.* (München 1935)

Ludendorff, E., *Meine Kriegserinnerungen 1914-1918* (Berlin 1920)

Ludendorff, E., *Tannenberg. Geschichtliche Wahrheit über die Schlacht* (München 1939) [1998]

Ludwig, E., *Hindenburg. Legende und Wirklichkeit* (Hamburg 1962)

Mahlberg, H., *Erich Ludendorff. Zum gedenken an seinen 100. Geburtstag* (hannover 1965)

Pierik,P/Pors, H., *De verlaten monarch. Keizer Wilhelm II in Nederland* (1999)

Rauchensteiner, M., *Der Tod des Doppeladlers. Oesterreich-Ungarn und der Erste Weltkrieg* (Wien 1993)
Rehwaldt, H., *Tannenberg* (Lengerich)
Reichsarchiv, (hg.), *Schlachten des Weltkrieges* Band 3 Antwerpen 1914 (Berlin 1925)
Reichsarchiv (hg.), *Schlachten des Weltkrieges* Band 19 Tannenberg (Berlin 1927)
Rosinski, H., *Die Deutsche Armee. Vom Triumph zur Niederlage* [1966] (München 1977)
Sasonoff, S.D., *Sechs schwere Jahre* (Berlin 1927)
Schaepdrijver, S. de, *De groote oorlog. Het koninkrijk België tijdens de Eerste Wereldoorlog* (Amsterdam 1997)
Schulze-Pfaelzer, G., *Hindenburg. Drie Zeitalter deutscher Nation* (Leipzig/Zürich 1930)
Schwarzmuller, T., *Zwischen Kaiser und 'Führer'. Generalfeldmarschall August von Mackensen. Eine politische Biographie* (Paderborn/München 1995)
Stone, N., *The Eastern Front 1914-1917* (London 1975)
Tschuppik, K., *Ludendorff. Die Tragödie des Fachmanns.* (Wien/Leipzig 1931)
Tuchman, B.W., *The Guns of August. August 1914* [1962] (London 1965)
Uhle-Wettler, F., *Erich Ludendorff in seiner Zeit. Soldat, Stratege, Revolutionär. Eine Neubewertung.* [1995] (Berg 1996)
Venohr, W., *Ludendorff. Legende und Wirklichkeit.* (Frankfurt am main 1993)
Wheeler-Bennett, J.W., *Hindenburg, the wooden Titan* [1939]
Werth, R. van, *Tannenberg. Wie Hindenburg die Russen schlug* (Berlin 1934)

Printed in Great Britain
by Amazon